The Sexually Dominant Woman

an illustrated workbook for
nervous beginners

by Janet W. Hardy

 greenery press

Readers should be aware that the activities and behaviors described in this book carry an inherent risk of physical and/or emotional injury. While we believe that following the guidelines set forth in this book will minimize that potential, the writer and publisher encourage you to be aware that you are taking some risk when you decide to engage in these activities, and to accept personal responsibility for that risk. In acting on the information in this book, you agree to accept that information as is and with all faults. Neither the author, the publisher, nor anyone else associated with the creation and sale of this book is responsible for any damage sustained.

CONTENTS

FOREWORD, by Midori

Hello!

I'm glad you found this book - because you and your partner are about to explore new pleasures, and you deserve good friends to help you along the way. The woman who created this book, both in its original form and in this graphic version, is a kind, reliable and practical guide for your journey ahead.

Are you totally new to kinky sexy fun? If so, this book is written for you!

If you already know how to use the tools, have some toys, are familiar with the terminologies and have even had some kink fun, then this book is not for you. For you, there are many excellent books in the Greenery Press catalog as well as other resources. (Hey, check out my books while you're at it!)

I wish I could sit down for tea with you and ask you what brought you here. Have you been curious about kink for a long time, or is this a newly sparked curiosity? Were you drawn in through a story or a video? Did a lover whisper secret desires to you? Was it something a friend commented or posted? We all come to these explorations from different places.

Over a cup of oolong, I would find out what you hope to experience. Do you want to enjoy a bit of naughtiness? Are you hoping to ignite new levels of passions and pleasures? Would you like to just feel less lost and baffled? Seeking ways to make your partner's fantasies a reality? Each woman and each lover comes with different hopes and wants.

Sitting with you, I'd ask you about what you're apprehensive about. What are your concerns? What scares you? Are you feeling overwhelmed by all the information that's online and elsewhere? I know it can be super-overwhelming. The other worries you have, what are they? All good people start with various trepidations and concerns.

Since we aren't able to sit down together today, this lovely little book will help you out, just like a sweet chat we'd have.

When I was first exploring doing kinky things with and to my lover, we only had the most vague ideas. It was a bit of tying each other up and shagging. I remember one romantic getaway where we used terry cloth belts from the hotel bathrobes. At other times, a bit of rough sex got more bitey and scratchy than usual. It felt exhilarating, but we didn't have the words to describe the thrill and sense of danger.

I remember visiting a former silver mining town in New Mexico with a lover. The wild-west history and lore fascinated me. With a few bits of fancy lingerie and feather or two in my hair, I pretended to be a bawdy saloon madam with a gentleman caller. I didn't come anything close to being dressed like a 19th century business-owning Western woman, but we didn't care - soon the lacy bits were strewn around the room anyway. I may have used the feather some way. I don't remember - it's all a blur now.

I think I was much less inhibited when I didn't know anything. Once I figured out that there are specialized tools for this sort of sex games, and had a sliver of a clue that there are "right ways" and "wrong ways" to use the tools and make these games, I hesitated. I questioned. I doubted. I got baffled.

There was that one evening when I was using a flogger on my lover. (You'll find out about "impact play" and floggers later in this book.) They moaned. They swayed. They gasped. They thrust their cute butt out to me.

All these were good for me and I understood they were having a good time. I felt like an erotic badass. Then a weird thing happened. They started to laugh. First, a chuckle. Then it grew into a full-bore rolling laugh. What was going on? Were they laughing at me? Did they think this was all stupid? My confidence was deeply shaken, just when I thought I was doing so well in pleasing both my sweetie and me. Upset, I reached out to a more experienced friend. She comforted me and then shed light on the situation.

"Honey, they're not laughing at you. They're just really high from all the good sensations. Sometimes people just do that, when they're overcharged with pleasure. You did good!"

If she hadn't helped me through that experience, and put things into context, I might have been plagued with doubt and lack of confidence for a long time. That's not a feel-good way to carry on.

We all can benefit from good practical advice and perspective based on real-life experiences.

I know you'll come across a lot of information and images online. Today is indeed the golden age of kink information. The problem is that there's simply too much information and you have sort through a deluge of material. Sadly a lot of what passes for information is untested, fantasy-based, inaccurate, or just made up. So please take things with a grain of salt. If something sounds too slick, too perfect, too... too *anything*.... it might be more imagined than instructional. I think fantasy and kinky fiction is great - but it's not educational. It's like trying to learn how to drive from a car chase movie.

Enjoy the fantasy! It's even more fun when you enjoy it with your partners. Talk about it and fantasize about it with your sweeties. Find out what about the fantasy you like, and let yourself get inspired. You can have a sexy chat or sext about the fantasy and see how you can make some realizable part of it an addition to your sex life.

Some people use the term "BDSM" for kink. Most people define that by simply expanding the acronym.

B = Bondage
D = Discipline or Dominance
S = Sadistic desires or desire for Submission
M = Masochistic wants or appetite for Mastery

But I actually don't find this definition all that useful to start with. (Yes, there will be more discussion and practical explanation of these words in the chapters to follow!)

So here's your Auntie Midori's definition of BDSM or kink sex:

It's about joyous childhood play, with adult sexual privilege and cool toys.

Or, to put it another way: playing cops-and-robbers with shagging!

That's why we call it "play."

To paraphrase the great Auntie Mame: Life is a playground, darling, and most poor folks are bored to death. So get playing!

Affectionately yours,
Midori
Founder, ForteFemme Women's Intensive

PREFACE, by Janet W. Hardy

Between 1992, when I wrote the first edition of this book, and today, there have been innumerable changes in kink and BDSM practice, as erotic adventurers discover new ways to make each other happy. However, the basics remain the same and always will: take care of yourselves and each other, and have fun together.

If you share this book with someone who has been playing for a number of years, they may tell you that my advice is very conservative. They're right. Because I want this book to be short, fun and easy to learn from, I'm not going to discuss all the risks and decisions that are available within the boundaries of safety and consent. For now, I strongly recommend that beginners stick within the guidelines I've given you here. As you get more experience and develop your knowledge and skills, you may choose to play outside these guidelines - with a full appreciation for the risks and rewards to be found there.

I'd like to acknowledge all the people I've played with and learned from through the decades, particularly Dossie and Jay. Special thanks to the beta readers who helped me notice everything from tiny typos to huge honking omissions, especially Ian, Max and Patricia.

This book is dedicated, of course, to my dear E.

INTRODUCTION

WHO AM I?

I'M JANET*. WHEN I WROTE THE FIRST EDITION OF THIS BOOK, BACK IN 1992, I WAS HETEROSEXUAL AND IN MY LATE 30S. NOW I'M IN MY EARLY 60S AND BI. BUT, AS I SAID THEN...

"ONE OF MY CHIEF PLEASURES IN LIFE HAS BEEN EXPLORING SEXUAL DOMINATION."

THAT WAS TRUE THEN, AND IT'S STILL TRUE.

* IF YOU READ THE EARLIER VERSIONS OF THIS BOOK, YOU'LL REMEMBER ME AS "LADY GREEN," THE PEN NAME I USED BACK THEN.

WHO ARE YOU?

THAT'S A TRICKIER QUESTION. YOU MAY BELIEVE – BECAUSE THE MEDIA TOLD YOU – THAT A SEXUALLY DOMINANT WOMAN LOOKS LIKE THIS.

A WOMAN WHO LOOKS LIKE THIS IS USUALLY A PROFESSIONAL DOMINANT, WHO EARNS MONEY BY PROVIDING DOMINANCE TO CLIENTS.

IN FACT, MOST OF THE HUNDREDS OF SEXUALLY DOMINANT WOMEN I'VE MET THROUGH THE YEARS HAVE LOOKED MORE LIKE THESE. WE'RE ALL DIFFERENT SHAPES, SIZES, AGES AND COLORS. WE MAY LOOK LIKE YOUR NEIGHBOR OR YOUR COWORKER OR YOUR FRIEND...

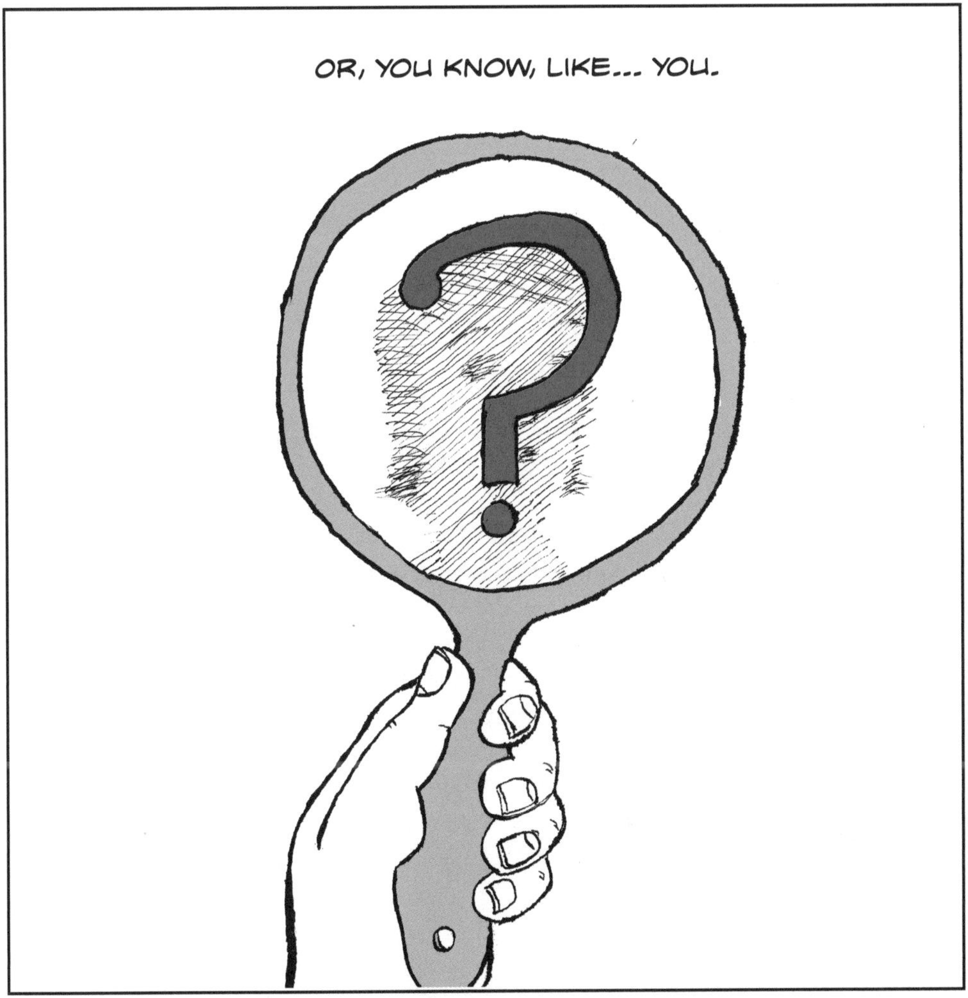
OR, YOU KNOW, LIKE... YOU.

IF YOU'VE EVER DREAMED OF BEING IN CONTROL
OF SOMEONE'S BEHAVIOR AND SEXUALITY...

IF YOU'VE EVER YEARNED TO HURT
SOMEONE, JUST A LITTLE...

IF THE IDEA OF HAVING SOMEONE TIED UP AND
HELPLESS MAKES YOU A BIT SHORT OF BREATH...

IF YOUR REGULAR, EVERYDAY SEX IS SEEMING
JUST A TAD BLAND AND BORING...

OR MAYBE EVEN IF YOU HAVE A PARTNER WHO
REALLY, REALLY WANTS THE EXPERIENCE OF SEXUAL
SUBMISSION THAT ONLY *YOU* CAN GIVE THEM...

THIS BOOK IS FOR YOU.

DO YOU WANT TO BE A SEXUALLY DOMINANT WOMAN?

BEFORE YOU READ ON, YOU SHOULD THINK THROUGH YOUR REASONS FOR WANTING TO BE SEXUALLY DOMINANT. THERE'S NO SINGLE ANSWER TO THIS QUESTION – EVERY WOMAN HAS DIFFERENT REASONS.

MAYBE YOU HAVE A PARTNER WHO REALLY WANTS THIS KIND OF PLAY.

MAYBE YOU HAVE FANTASIES OF SEXUAL DOMINATION, BUT NO ONE TO PLAY WITH.

YOU MAY BE FASCINATED BY SEXUAL DOMINATION BUT UNSURE HOW TO PROCEED.

OR MAYBE YOU'VE ALWAYS BEEN SUBMISSIVE,
AND ARE BEGINNING TO WONDER WHAT THE OTHER
SIDE OF THE EQUATION MIGHT BE LIKE.

WHAT DO YOU HOPE TO GAIN?

MAKE NO MISTAKE ABOUT IT, SEXUAL DOMINATION IS A LOT OF WORK AND RESPONSIBILITY. IF IT WEREN'T FOR ITS MANY REWARDS, I DOUBT PEOPLE WOULD BOTHER WITH IT. BUT THERE *ARE* REWARDS, AND THEY CAN BE PRETTY FABULOUS.

MAYBE YOUR SUBMISSIVE PARTNER CAN FIND JOY IN HELPING YOU WITH YOUR EVERYDAY TASKS.

MAYBE YOU CAN GET THE PHYSICAL NURTURING AND CARE YOU'VE BEEN CRAVING.

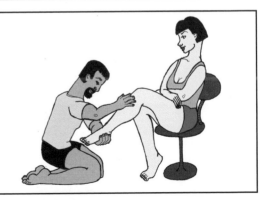

PERHAPS YOU'D ENJOY HAVING THE CHANCE TO APPLY A LITTLE... MOTIVATION.

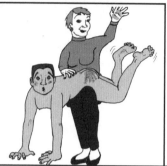

OR YOU'RE READY TO GET *EXACTLY* WHAT YOU WANT IN BED.

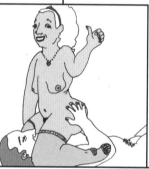

OR YOU'D LIKE TO EXPERIENCE BEING THE BELLE OF THE BALL (GOOD FEMALE DOMINANTS ARE FEW AND FAR BETWEEN).

ALL THESE, AND MORE, ARE
EXCELLENT REASONS TO TRY
SEXUAL DOMINATION.

IT'S PERFECTLY NORMAL TO FEEL NERVOUS ABOUT THE IDEA OF DOMINATING SOMEONE. THAT'S JUST A SIGN THAT YOU'RE TAKING DOMINATION AS SERIOUSLY AS IT DESERVES.

THERE *ARE* SOME TECHNICAL SKILLS YOU'LL NEED TO LEARN. THEY'RE NOT AS COMPLICATED AS THEY SEEM, BUT YOU'LL STILL NEED TO GIVE THEM CAREFUL ATTENTION AND PRACTICE.

STILL NOT FEELING IT? READ ON – YOU MAY DISCOVER THAT SOME TYPES OF DOMINATION DO HOLD A CHARGE FOR YOU. BUT IF YOU REALLY, TRULY DON'T FEEL LIKE DOING SEXUAL DOMINATION, DON'T LET ANYBODY PUSH YOU INTO IT.*

* IF YOU AREN'T INTERESTED IN DOMINATION, BUT YOU HAVE A PARTNER WHO WANTS IT, LOOK IN THE RESOURCE GUIDE AT THE BACK. THERE YOU'LL FIND MY SUGGESTIONS FOR BOOKS AND OTHER RESOURCES THAT CAN HELP YOU FIND A WAY TO MANAGE THIS DIFFERENCE.

REMEMBER,
DOMINANCE
DOESN'T REQUIRE
THT YOU LOOK
A CERTAIN WAY
OR DRESS A
CERTAIN WAY.

CONFIDENCE
DOES HELP,
THOUGH. SO
DOES A SENSE
OF HUMOR.

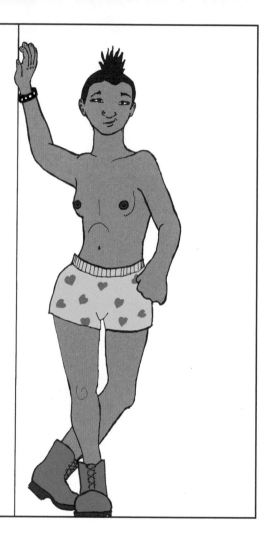

12

IF YOU WANT TO GO FURTHER...

DOES THE WHOLE IDEA OF DOMINANCE MAKE YOU FEEL A LITTLE BASHFUL? THIS IS THE BOOK FOR YOU: *EXHIBITIONISM FOR THE SHY* BY CAROL QUEEN, PUBLISHED BY DOWN THERE PRESS.

MIDORI TEACHES WEEKEND-LONG, SMALL-GROUP CLASSES FOR WOMEN WISHING TO ACCESS THEIR AUTHENTIC POWER, INSIDE THE BEDROOM AND OUTSIDE IT. VISIT *WWW. FORTEFEMME.COM* FOR MORE INFO.

WHAT KIND OF DOMME*
DO YOU WANT TO BE?

THERE ARE AS MANY WAYS TO BE A DOMINANT WOMAN
AS THERE ARE DOMINANT WOMEN – WHICH IS TO
SAY, A LOT. HOWEVER, MOST DOMINANCE FALLS INTO
ONE OR MORE OF SIX BASIC CATEGORIES.

AS YOU READ ABOUT THE DIFFERENT FLAVORS OF DOMINANCE,
TRY TO IMAGINE YOURSELF DOING THEM. THE ONES THAT INTEREST
OR AROUSE YOU ARE THE ONES YOU'LL WANT TO PURSUE.

SOME OF US SEE APPEAL IN MORE THAN ONE CATEGORY.
SOME OF US WILL HAVE PARTNERS WHO ARE INTERESTED IN A
DIFFERENT CATEGORY, AND WILL THUS HAVE TO FIGURE OUT KINDS
OF PLAY THAT APPEAL TO BOTH OURSELVES AND OUR PARTNERS.

YES, I KNOW IT SEEMS AS THOUGH THE DOMINANT SHOULD
ALWAYS GET HER WAY, BUT DOMINANCE IS A LOT TRICKIER THAN
THAT. REMEMBER, YOU WANT TO BE ABLE TO PLAY WITH THEM
MORE THAN ONCE, WHICH MEANS YOU NEED THEM TO COME
BACK FOR MORE – AND FEW WILL DO THAT IF THEY DIDN'T
GET THEIR BASIC NEEDS MET DURING THE FIRST SCENE.

---

* A SHORTER WAY OF SAYING "FEMALE DOMINANT." IT'S PRONOUNCED "DOM"
(NOT "DOM-MAY"). ANOTHER SHORTHAND IS "FEMDOM" OR "FEMDOMME."

SERVICE

IN THIS KIND OF DOMINANCE, THE SUB PLEASES THE DOMME BY TAKING CARE OF ONE OR MORE OF HER NEEDS. SERVICE CAN RANGE FROM HOUSEKEEPING AND CLERICAL CHORES TO SEXUAL SERVICE, AND BEYOND.

SENSATION

IF YOUR FANTASIES OF DOMINATION INCLUDE
GIVING YOUR PARTNER INTENSE OR PAINFUL
SENSATIONS, THIS STYLE IS FOR YOU.
SENSATION CAN BE GIVEN AS PART OF
EROTIC PLAY, AS "FUNISHMENT,"* AS A
WAY OF ACHIEVING AN ECSTATIC STATE, AS
AN EMOTIONAL RELEASE, AND MORE.

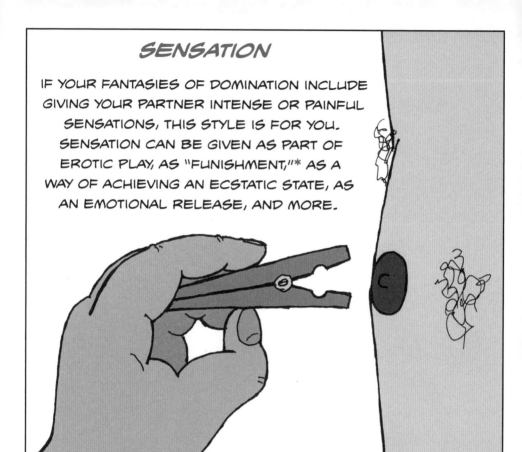

* STRONG SENSATION GIVEN AS PART OF A "NAUGHTINESS"
ROLEPLAY SCENARIO, PURELY FOR EROTIC FUN.

BONDAGE

BONDAGE INVOLVES
TYING YOUR PARTNER
SO THAT THEY
FEEL A SENSE OF
HELPLESSNESS AND
YOU FEEL A SENSE
OF POWER. YOU
DON'T NEED TO BE A
FORMER GIRL SCOUT
– GOOD BONDAGE
REQUIRES ONLY A
COUPLE OF EASY-TO-
LEARN KNOTS. OR, IF
KNOTS AREN'T YOUR
THING, INVEST IN SOME
GOOD RESTRAINTS.

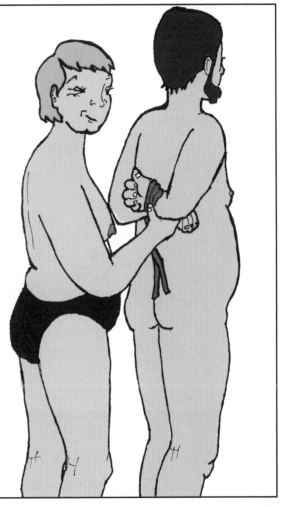

17

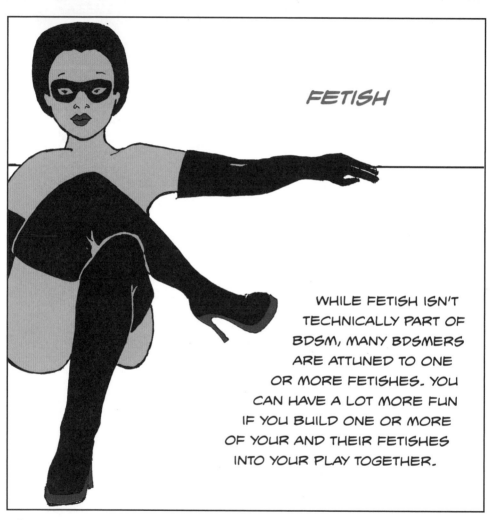

FETISH

WHILE FETISH ISN'T
TECHNICALLY PART OF
BDSM, MANY BDSMERS
ARE ATTUNED TO ONE
OR MORE FETISHES. YOU
CAN HAVE A LOT MORE FUN
IF YOU BUILD ONE OR MORE
OF YOUR AND THEIR FETISHES
INTO YOUR PLAY TOGETHER.

ROLE-PLAY

IF YOU HAVE A YEN FOR THE THEATRICAL, ROLE-PLAY MAY BE FOR YOU. YOU AND YOUR PARTNER CAN SPEND YOUR TIME AS A SCHOOLMISTRESS WITH AN UNRULY STUDENT, A CONQUEROR WITH A NEW SLAVE, AN INTERROGATOR WITH A STUBBORN CAPTIVE, OR ANYTHING ELSE YOUR IMAGINATION CAN CONCEIVE.

IF YOU WANT TO GO FURTHER...

MISTRESS LORELEI POWERS'S *THE MISTRESS MANUAL* IS PARTICULARLY HELPFUL FOR FIGURING OUT THE ARCHETYPES THAT DETERMINE THE "FLAVOR" OF YOUR SCENE OR RELATIONSHIP.

JAY WISEMAN'S *SM 101: A REALISTIC INTRODUCTION* IS ESPECIALLY STRONG ON BASICS AND SAFETY INFORMATION. THE AUTHOR IS A SWITCHABLE MALE DOMINANT WITH INSIGHTS FOR PLAYERS OF ALL GENDERS.

JOHN AND LIBBY WARREN'S *THE LOVING DOMINANT* IS ORIENTED TOWARD MALE-DOM RELATIONSHIPS, BUT AT LEAST 90% OF ITS INFORMATION IS USEFUL TO DOMINANTS OF ANY GENDER OR ORIENTATION.

FUNDAMENTALS: SAFETY & CONSENT

THE REASON PEOPLE BUY AND READ BOOKS LIKE THIS IS THAT KINK HAS A BUILT-IN SET OF PHYSICAL AND EMOTIONAL RISKS – AND LEARNING HOW TO MANAGE THOSE RISKS IS ESSENTIAL TO BEING A RESPONSIBLE PLAYER.

AT FIRST, SOME OF THESE PROCESSES WILL FEEL A LITTLE UNNATURAL – FEW OF US GREW UP WITH GOOD MODELS FOR TALKING ABOUT SEX. FINDING OUT AHEAD OF TIME ABOUT WHAT EACH OF YOU WANTS AND DOES NOT WANT GETS EASIER WITH PRACTICE, THOUGH.

KINKSTERS CALL SUCH CONVERSATIONS "NEGOTIATION," WHICH MAKES THEM SOUND DULL. IN FACT, THEY CAN BE ANYTHING BUT. I PREFER TO THINK OF THEM AS "COLLABORATIVE PLANNING," IN WHICH EACH OF YOU CAN SHARE YOUR FANTASIES, DESIRES AND LIMITS SO THAT YOU CAN CRAFT A SCENE THAT WILL BE AS MUCH FUN AS POSSIBLE FOR BOTH OF YOU.

NEGOTIATION CAN FEEL VERY VULNERABLE, THOUGH. I STRONGLY SUGGEST YOU START WITH AN AGREEMENT THAT NEITHER OF YOU WILL LAUGH AT, OR ACT GROSSED OUT BY, THE OTHER'S DESIRES.

21

IF YOU FEEL STUCK ABOUT WHAT KINDS OF THINGS YOU CAN NEGOTIATE, YOU CAN FIND LONG, DETAILED LISTS IN BOOKS AND ON THE INTERNET. HOWEVER, MANY SEX THERAPISTS PREFER AN EXERCISE CALLED "YES/NO/MAYBE."

BOTH OF YOU SIT DOWN WITH A BIG SHEET OF PAPER AND BRAINSTORM EVERYTHING TWO PEOPLE CAN POSSIBLY DO IN SEX OR KINK. DON'T HOLD BACK. THEN, EACH OF YOU TAKES A DIFFERENT COLORED PEN AND MARKS EACH ITEM WITH A "Y" FOR "YES," AN "N" FOR "NO," OR AN "M" FOR "MAYBE."

A "NO" FROM EITHER OF YOU MEANS THAT ACTIVITY IS OFF THE TABLE FOR NOW, WITHOUT ARGUMENT. YOU CAN ALWAYS REVISIT THE LIST LATER TO SEE IF ANYONE'S FEELINGS HAVE CHANGED.

"MAYBE" MEANS "IF I WERE TURNED ON ENOUGH" OR "IF IT FELT SAFE ENOUGH" OR "IF YOU WARM ME UP FIRST" OR WHATEVER. THESE ARE THE ITEMS YOU NEED TO DISCUSS.

23

THE LIST OF "Y" AND "M"
ANSWERS IS THE BLUEPRINT FOR
YOUR SCENES TOGETHER.

YOU SHOULD REACH AN AGREEMENT ABOUT HOW TO LET EACH OTHER KNOW IF SOMETHING GOES WRONG. IF YOU'RE NOT INTO PRETEND NONCONSENT, A SIMPLE "STOP" OR "NO" WORKS FINE. BUT IF YOUR PARTNER LIKES TO BE ABLE TO SHOUT "NO STOP PLEASE" WITHOUT ENDING THE SCENE, YOU'LL NEED A SAFEWORD.*

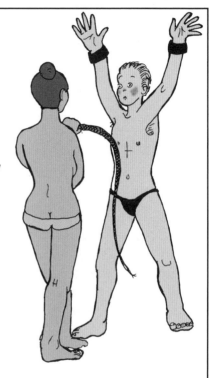

A SAFEWORD CAN BE ANY WORD OR SIGNAL THAT WOULDN'T ORDINARILY COME UP DURING PLAY. MANY KINKSTERS USE "RED" TO MEAN "STOP RIGHT NOW," "YELLOW" TO MEAN "PLEASE SLOW DOWN OR EASE UP," AND "GREEN" TO MEAN "ALL SYSTEMS GO!" AND REMEMBER, SAFEWORDS AREN'T JUST FOR SUBS – A DOMINANT CAN GET TRIGGERED, OVERWHELMED OR SICK, AND THAT MEANS YOU NEED A SAFEWORD TOO.

* IF NO SAFEWORD HAS BEEN NEGOTIATED, "NO" AND "STOP" AND OTHER WORDS OF THAT TYPE MEAN THAT THE SCENE IS OVER. NO EXCEPTIONS.

DO NOT TRY TO DO SEXUAL DOMINANCE IF EITHER
YOU OR YOUR PARTNER IS INTOXICATED OR HIGH.
THE VAST MAJORITY OF KINK ACCIDENTS AND
CONSENT VIOLATIONS HAPPEN WHEN ONE OR
BOTH PLAYERS HAS BEEN USING INTOXICANTS.

THROUGHOUT THE BOOK, I'LL MENTION
SPECIFIC SAFETY CONCERNS AND
WAYS TO MINIMIZE RISKS ON PAGES
THAT LOOK LIKE THIS. PLEASE PAY
SPECIAL ATTENTION TO THESE.

FUNDAMENTALS: BONDAGE

IT MIGHT SEEM LIKE "BONDAGE IS BONDAGE." BUT ACTUALLY, PEOPLE DO BONDAGE FOR A NUMBER OF REASONS.

SOME PEOPLE LIKE *RESTRICTIVE* BONDAGE – THE KIND THAT FEELS LIKE THEY CAN'T GET OUT UNLESS YOU UNTIE THEM.

OTHERS LIKE *DECORATIVE* BONDAGE, THAT SETS OFF THEIR BEST FEATURES IN A HANDSOME FRAME OF ROPE.

BONDAGE CAN BE USED FOR *SENSATION,* HUGGING TIGHT AGAINST SENSITIVE BITS AND MAKING THEM TINGLE.

BONDAGE CAN BE USED IN *ROLEPLAYING:* PIRATES AND SAILORS, SOLDIERS AND CAPTIVES, COPS AND ROBBERS – WHATEVER NARRATIVE TAKES YOUR FANCY.

IT'S IMPORTANT TO DISCUSS YOUR GOALS AHEAD OF TIME. OTHERWISE, IT MIGHT BE THAT YOUR PARTNER NEEDS VERY RESTRICTIVE BONDAGE TO FEEL SECURE, AND YOU'VE JUST CAREFULLY KNOTTED A FULL-BODY DECORATIVE HARNESS THAT DOESN'T IMPEDE THEIR MOVEMENT AT ALL. I'M SURE YOU CAN SEE THE PROBLEM.

BUT FIRST, LET'S DISCUSS SAFETY.

MANY PEOPLE THINK OF BONDAGE AS AN "EASY," ENTRY-LEVEL KINK ACTIVITY. BUT IT'S RISKIER THAN MANY OTHER FORMS OF KINK – WHICH SIMPLY MEANS THAT YOU NEED TO SPEND A LITTLE BIT OF TIME AND EFFORT LEARNING HOW TO DO IT SAFELY AND WELL.

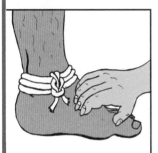

TO BE SURE THAT YOU'RE NOT CUTTING OFF CIRCULATION ANYWHERE, CHECK THE BOUND PART PERIODICALLY FOR COLDNESS AND NUMBNESS.

CONSIDER ACQUIRING A SET OF RESTRAINTS. NYLON ONES ARE AVAILABLE IN EROTIC BOUTIQUES AND ON THE INTERNET, AND ARE QUITE AFFORDABLE.

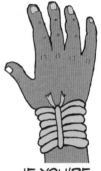

IF YOU'RE WORKING WITH ROPE, MAKE SURE THAT YOU SPREAD THE PRESSURE OVER A WIDE ENOUGH AREA. I'LL EXPLAIN HOW ON P. 40.

DO NOT PLACE BONDAGE ACROSS THE FRONT OF ANYONE'S NECK.

AVOID PLACING BONDAGE OVER PLACES ON THE BODY WHERE THERE IS LITTLE FAT OR MUSCLE PROTECTING SKIN AND NERVES. MOST JOINTS ARE NOT GOOD PLACES FOR BONDAGE.

NOPE →

ONE PLACE TO BE ESPECIALLY CAREFUL IS THE UNPROTECTED "NOTCH" BETWEEN THE WRISTBONE AND THE BASE OF THE THUMB.

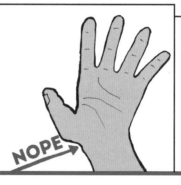

DO NOT USE STOCKINGS, OR ANYTHING STRETCHY, FOR BONDAGE. STOCKINGS CAN TIGHTEN DOWN INTO A NARROW, ABRASIVE SURFACE THAT CAN CUT INTO SKIN. IN GENERAL, IF YOU USE ANY HOUSEHOLD ITEM FOR BONDAGE, BE PREPARED TO CUT IT OFF — SO IF YOU DON'T WANT TO CUT IT OFF, DON'T USE IT.

I DON'T RECOMMEND HANDCUFFS, EITHER. THE EDGE OF THE CUFF CAN PRESS INTO THE BASE OF THE THUMB AND DAMAGE THE NERVES THERE. IF YOU DECIDE TO TRY HANDCUFFS, BUY REAL ONES WITH DOUBLE LOCKS TO PREVENT THEM FROM TIGHTENING, AND USE THE DOUBLE LOCKS.

AND NEVER, EVER LEAVE A HELPLESS BOUND PERSON ALONE FOR MORE THAN A QUICK RUN TO THE BATHROOM.

31

ALWAYS HAVE THE PROPER TOOLS ON HAND TO RELEASE SOMEONE QUICKLY IN CASE OF EMERGENCIES.* FOR ROPE AND LIGHT RESTRAINTS, "PARAMEDIC SHEARS" – WHICH ARE MEANT TO CUT THROUGH SEATBELTS AND OTHER TOUGH MATERIALS – WORK GREAT. IF YOU'RE USING TOYS WITH LOCKS, GET A LOCKSMITH TO KEY THEM ALL TO THE SAME KEY, AND KEEP A BACKUP KEY IN A SAFE, MEMORABLE PLACE. IF YOU'RE USING CHAINS OR CUFFS, GET BOLT CUTTERS.

* NOT JUST PLAY EMERGENCIES. IF THERE WERE AN EARTHQUAKE, TORNADO OR FIRE WHEN YOUR PARTNER IS IN BONDAGE, HOW LONG WOULD IT TAKE YOU TO GET THEM OUT?

GAGS CAN BE FUN, BUT THEY CARRY
SOME EXTRA RISKS. FIRST, YOU MUST
MAKE SURE THAT YOUR PARTNER HAS
SOME WAY TO COMMUNICATE THAT
THEY NEED THE SCENE TO CHANGE
OR STOP. IF YOU'RE USING A GAG, BE
SURE TO AGREE ON A NON-VERBAL
SAFEWORD, SUCH AS THREE GRUNTS, A
SQUEAKY TOY, OR A RING OF KEYS THAT
WILL MAKE A SOUND IF DROPPED.

NEVER, EVER USE A GAG THAT YOUR
PARTNER COULD INHALE OR SWALLOW.
ANY MOUTH STUFFING MUST BE ATTACHED
TO THE PART THAT TIES AROUND YOUR
PARTNER'S HEAD, WITH AN ATTACHMENT
TOO STURDY TO BE BITTEN THROUGH.

MANY COMMERCIAL GAGS ARE TOO LARGE
FOR MOST MOUTHS. IF YOU BUY A GAG,
START SMALL. AND BEFORE USING A GAG,
MAKE SURE YOUR PARTNER'S NOSE IS
NOT TOO STUFFY TO BREATHE THROUGH.

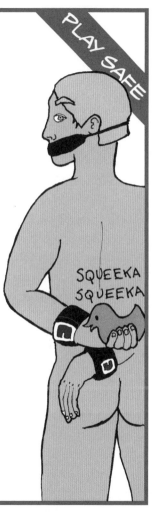

SQUEEKA
SQUEEKA

BLINDFOLDS ARE USEFUL IN MANY WAYS: TO CALM DOWN A SUBMISSIVE WHO'S FEELING GIGGLY OR JUMPY... TO ADD TO A FEELING OF HELPLESSNESS... TO INCREASE FOCUS ON SENSATIONS BY TAKING AWAY THE SENSE OF SIGHT.

BLINDFOLDS ARE ALSO A HUGE HELP TO A DOMINANT WHO'S NOT YET TOTALLY CONFIDENT. ONCE YOUR SUB IS BLINDFOLDED, THEY CAN'T SEE YOU FUMBLING, BEING NERVOUS... OR TAKING OFF THOSE HIGH HEELS TO MAKE YOURSELF COMFORTABLE.

HOWEVER, A BLINDFOLDED SUB IS VERY DEPENDENT ON YOU. DO NOT TRY TO MOVE THEM UNLESS YOU'RE GUIDING THEM WITH YOUR HANDS, AND BE EXTRA-ALERT TO ANY LOSS OF BALANCE, ESPECIALLY IF THEIR HANDS AND/OR LEGS ARE TIED.

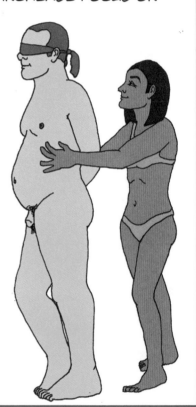

RESTRICTIVE BONDAGE

THIS IS THE TYPE MOST PEOPLE THINK OF WHEN THEY TALK ABOUT BONDAGE – THE KIND THAT RESTRICTS MOVEMENT AND THAT FEELS LIKE THEY CAN'T ESCAPE. COULD THEY REALLY ESCAPE IF THEY WANTED TO? – THAT DEPENDS ON THEIR FLEXIBILITY AND STRENGTH. BUT IF YOU'RE DOING THIS KIND OF BONDAGE, IT SHOULD *FEEL LIKE* THEY'RE IN IT UNTIL YOU DECIDE TO LET THEM OUT.

SOME STUBBORN PARTNERS WILL STRUGGLE SO HARD AGAINST THE BONDAGE THAT THEY HURT THEMSELVES. IF YOU THINK THAT MAY BE WHAT'S HAPPENING, STOP THE SCENE. PULLED MUSCLES AND STRAINED JOINTS ARE NOT GOOD ACCESSORIES FOR PLAY.

DECORATIVE BONDAGE

DECORATIVE BONDAGE IS THE EXACT OPPOSITE OF INESCAPABLE BONDAGE: IT'S THERE TO BE PRETTY, NOT TO HOLD YOUR PARTNER IN PLACE. YOU CAN USE DECORATIVE BONDAGE TO ACCENTUATE YOUR FAVORITE PARTS OF YOUR PARTNER'S BODY. SOME PEOPLE MAKE BONDAGE INTO AN ART, INTERWEAVING MULTICOLORED ROPES AND DECORATIVE OBJECTS. DECORATIVE BONDAGE CAN BE COLLABORATIVE, WITH YOU AND YOUR PARTNER DECIDING TOGETHER THAT *THIS* ROPE WOULD LOOK REALLY BEAUTIFUL ACROSS *THAT* BODY PART. SINCE YOU'RE COLLABORATING, YOU CAN EXCHANGE INFORMATION ABOUT WHAT FEELS GOOD AND WHAT LOOKS NICE, WHICH IS A GREAT WAY TO LEARN.

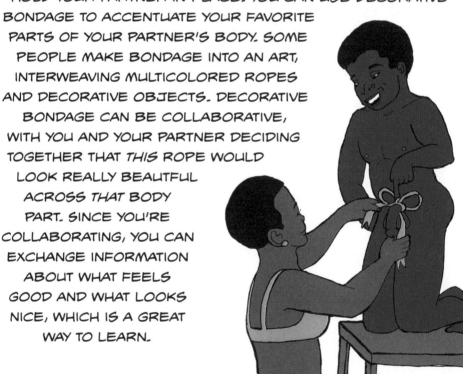

BONDAGE FOR SENSATION

BONDAGE OFFERS A COMBINATION OF PRESSURE AND CONSTRICTION. APPLIED TO A SENSITIVE BODY PART, IT CAN HEIGHTEN OTHER SENSATIONS LIKE CLAMPS OR IMPACT, OR BE A SENSATION ALL BY ITSELF.

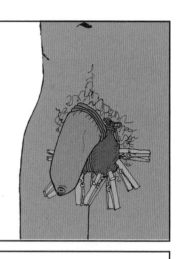

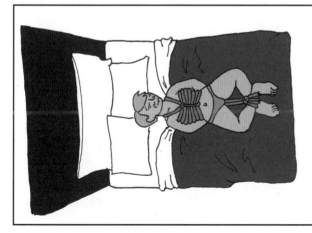

SOME PEOPLE LOVE BONDAGE THAT MAKES THEM FEEL "SWADDLED," LIKE A BABY IN A BLANKET. THEY MAY DRIFT OFF INTO A PEACEFUL, SERENE STATE.

ROLEPLAY BONDAGE

BONDAGE CAN BE AN ADJUNCT TO MANY DIFFERENT ROLEPLAYING SCENARIOS. IF YOU WANT TO PLAY AS A PIRATE, COWGIRL, COP, CRIMINAL, OR... LET YOUR IMAGINATION BE YOUR GUIDE... A FEW WELL-PLACED ROPES OR RESTRAINTS WILL HELP MAKE YOUR SCENE SING.

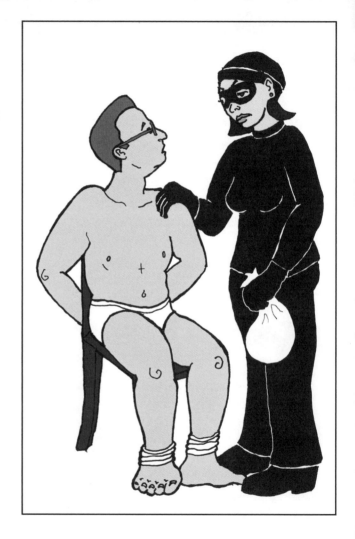

BASIC BONDAGE PRINCIPLES

THE FIRST THING TO REMEMBER ABOUT BONDAGE IS THAT PRESSURE APPLIED TO A NARROW AREA IS MUCH MORE DANGEROUS THAN THE SAME PRESSURE SPREAD OUT.

IF YOU'RE USING RESTRAINTS, THAT PROBLEM IS TAKEN CARE OF SIMPLY BY THE STRUCTURE OF THE RESTRAINTS. LEATHER RESTRAINTS ARE SEXY AND FUN, BUT ALSO PRICEY. FORTUNATELY, RESTRAINTS OF NYLON OR CANVAS ARE CHEAPER AND WORK JUST AS WELL.*

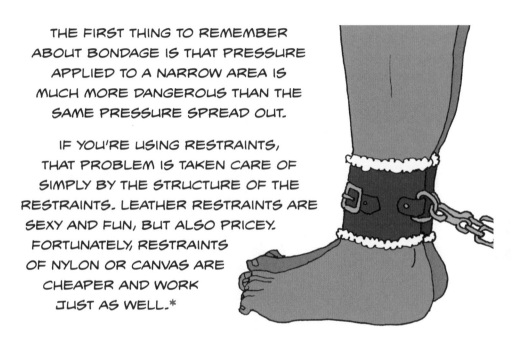

* A BIGGER INVESTMENT, BUT A GREAT TOY FOR BEGINNERS, IS SPORTSHEETS® – FITTED SHEETS MADE OF THE SOFT SIDE OF VELCRO, PAIRED WITH RESTRAINTS THAT FEATURE THE HOOK SIDE. YOU CAN SIMPLY STICK YOUR PARTNER DOWN IN WHATEVER POSITION PLEASES YOU.

IF YOU'RE USING ROPE, SIMPLY WRAPPING IT SEVERAL TIMES AROUND YOUR PARTNER'S LIMB DOESN'T SOLVE THE PROBLEM.

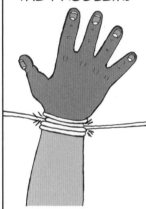

THE STRAND THAT HAS THE MOST PRESSURE ON IT WILL TIGHTEN DOWN AND CAUSE PROBLEMS.

INSTEAD, TWIST THE ENDS TOGETHER, PASS ONE OF THEM UNDER ALL YOUR STRANDS, AND TIE A SQUARE KNOT OVER THE WHOLE THING. TO TIE TWO LIMBS TOGETHER, USE THE SAME PRINCIPLE: MAKE SEVERAL WRAPS AROUND BOTH LIMBS, THEN TWIST THE ENDS TOGETHER BETWEEN THE LIMBS, PASS THEM AROUND ALL THE STRANDS, AND TIE OFF.

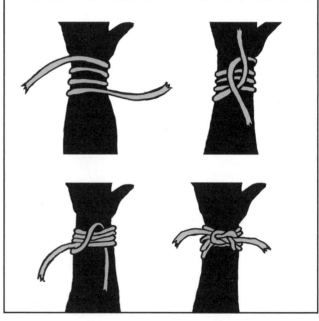

MANY DOMINANT WOMEN AVOID DOING BONDAGE BECAUSE THEY DON'T KNOW HOW TO TIE FANCY KNOTS. BUT GOOD BONDAGE REQUIRES ONLY TWO OR THREE SIMPLE KNOTS.*

THE LARKSHEAD IS USEFUL FOR ATTACHING TO INANIMATE OBJECTS LIKE BEDPOSTS, OR AS THE STARTING POINT FOR A WRAPPED SERIES OF STRANDS. SIMPLY FOLD YOUR ROPE IN HALF AND PASS THE FREE ENDS BACK THROUGH THE LOOP.

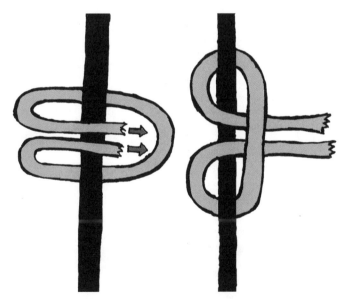

* IF YOU HAVE AS MUCH TROUBLE WITH SPATIAL RELATIONS AS I DO, *THE KLUTZ BOOK OF KNOTS* IS A GREAT RESOURCE FOR HANDS-ON PRACTICE.

IF YOU WERE A SCOUT, YOU MAY ALREADY KNOW HOW TO TIE A SQUARE KNOT. IF NOT, THE MNEMONIC IS, "RIGHT OVER LEFT, LEFT OVER RIGHT, MAKES THE KNOT NEAT AND TIDY AND TIGHT." IF YOU DON'T DO IT THAT WAY, YOUR KNOT MAY BE A GRANNY KNOT, WHICH CAN SLIDE EITHER TOO LOOSE OR TOO TIGHT.

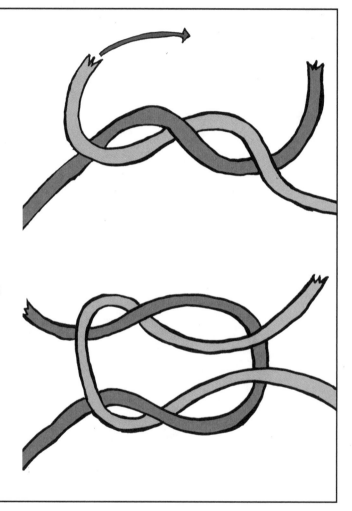

ANOTHER USEFUL KNOT TO KNOW IS TWO HALF-HITCHES, WHICH IS GOOD FOR ATTACHING THE END OF THE ROPE TO A STATIONARY OBJECT LIKE A BEAM OR BEDPOST. DON'T USE IT ON HUMAN PARTS, THOUGH, AS IT'S DESIGNED TO TIGHTEN UNDER PRESSURE.

43

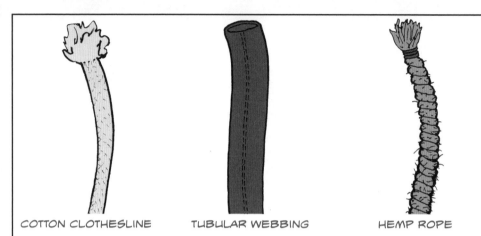

COTTON CLOTHESLINE   TUBULAR WEBBING   HEMP ROPE

IF YOU WANT TO TRY ROPE, YOU'LL FIND THAT IT COMES IN ALL SIZES, COLORS AND TEXTURES. MOST BONDAGE PRACTITIONERS PREFER ROPE 1/4" TO 3/8" (6-8MM) THICK. PURE COTTON CLOTHESLINE IS A GOOD CHOICE FOR BEGINNERS - NOT SO SLIPPERY THAT YOUR KNOTS WILL FALL OUT, BUT SMOOTH ENOUGH NOT TO ABRADE SKIN IF USED PROPERLY. I AM A FAN OF THE TUBULAR WEBBING SOLD IN CLIMBING STORES, WHICH IS SMOOTH, EASY TO TIE, AND PRETTY. PURISTS PREFER HEMP FOR ITS SCRATCHY TEXTURE AND CLASSIC LOOK - IF YOU'RE INTERESTED, I SUGGEST GETTING YOUR FIRST BATCH FROM ONE OF THE SEVERAL BUSINESSES WHICH CUT, DYE AND PREPARE HEMP ROPES SPECIFICALLY FOR BONDAGE.

IF YOU THINK
BONDAGE IS GOING
TO BE AN ONGOING
ACTIVITY, CONSIDER
ADDING SOME
ATTACHMENT POINTS
TO YOUR PLAY
AREA. IF YOU HAVE
PRIVACY CONCERNS,
EYE BOLTS CAN BE
ATTACHED BETWEEN
THE FRAME AND
THE MATTRESS
OF A WOODEN
BEDFRAME. IF YOU
WANT ATTACHMENTS
IN YOUR WALL OR
CEILING, BUT ARE
NOT 100% CERTAIN
OF YOUR ABILITY
TO CENTER A BOLT
INTO A STUD OR JOIST, HAVE IT DONE BY A PROFESSIONAL
HANDYPERSON OR OTHER EXPERIENCED INDIVIDUAL.

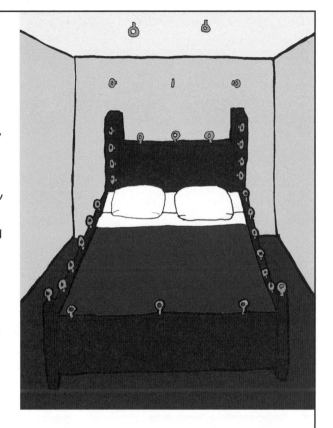

IF YOU WANT TO GO FURTHER...

IF BONDAGE TURNS OUT TO BE AN IMPORTANT KINK FOR YOU OR YOUR PARTNER, I STRONGLY ENCOURAGE YOU TO ACQUIRE ONE OR MORE OF THESE BOOKS – THERE'S A LOT MORE TO LEARN THAN I CAN OFFER HERE.

JAY WISEMAN'S EROTIC BONDAGE HANDBOOK, BY JAY WISEMAN

BONDAGE FOR SEX, BY CHANTA ROSE

THE SEDUCTIVE ART OF JAPANESE BONDAGE, BY MIDORI

SHIBARI YOU CAN USE: JAPANESE ROPE BONDAGE AND EROTIC MACRAMÉ, BY LEE HARRINGTON

FUNDAMENTALS: SENSATION

IF YOU LOOK FOR PHOTOS OF SEXUALLY DOMINANT WOMEN, YOU'LL FIND A LOT OF PICTURES OF LEATHER-CLAD WOMEN HOLDING BULLWHIPS OR RIDING CROPS. MAYBE THAT'S WHY MANY PEOPLE THINK KINKY PLAY ALWAYS INVOLVES PAIN. IT DOESN'T - FOR TWO REASONS.

FIRST, A LOT OF PEOPLE ENJOY STYLES OF PLAY THAT DON'T INCLUDE STRONG SENSATION OF ANY KIND.

SECOND, WHEN YOUR PARTNER IS AROUSED OR EXCITED BY YOUR PLAY, THEY MIGHT FEEL KEEN PLEASURE FROM SENSATIONS THAT WOULD BE PAINFUL AT OTHER TIMES.

AND, OF COURSE, SOME PEOPLE *DO* LIKE TO PLAY WITH PAIN - TO PROVE THEIR STRENGTH, TO GET TURNED ON, TO FIND EMOTIONAL RELEASE IN YELLING OR TEARS, TO REACH AN ECSTATIC STATE.

NO MATTER WHERE YOU FALL IN THOSE GROUPS, IT'S WORTH YOUR WHILE TO LEARN A LITTLE ABOUT THE INTENSE SENSATIONS WE PLAY WITH IN KINK - WHEN AND HOW TO GIVE THEM, AND HOW TO DO SO SAFELY.

IMPACT

PERHAPS THE MOST COMMON FORM OF SENSATION PLAY
IS IMPACT PLAY — SPANKING, FLOGGING, SLAPPING, ETC.

THERE ARE ALL KINDS OF REASONS THAT YOUR SCENE
MIGHT INCLUDE SOME IMPACT. YOU MIGHT BE DOING
"FUNISHMENT" (SEE P. 55). YOU MIGHT BE DOING A ROLEPLAY
THAT INCLUDES IMPACT: A LADIES' MAID WITH A STRICT
EMPLOYER, AN ATHLETE WITH A COACH, A COCKY TEENAGER
WITH A DISAPPROVING AUNT... WELL, YOU GET THE IDEA.

SOME PEOPLE CAN GET OFF ON IMPACT: IT'S NOT TOO
RARE FOR SOMEONE TO BE ABLE TO REACH ORGASM
FROM STROKES PROPERLY APPLIED — AND EVEN THOSE
WHO CAN'T QUITE REACH ORGASM CAN NONETHELESS
GET VERY TURNED ON. OTHERS MAY NOT REACT SEXUALLY,
BUT MAY NEVERTHELESS FIND THAT IMPACT CAN TAKE
THEM INTO A DREAMY OR EVEN ECSTATIC STATE, OR
ALLOW THEM TO RELEASE PENT-UP EMOTIONS.

AS IN ALL KINKY PLAY, TALK WITH YOUR PARTNER FIRST TO MAKE
SURE YOU'RE ON THE SAME PAGE. IF THEY THINK THEY'RE
RECEIVING A CUTE NAUGHTY "FUNISHMENT," AND YOU THINK
YOU'RE A STERN TASKMISTRESS WHO IS GOING TO GIVE THEM
THE WHALING OF THEIR LIFE, THINGS ARE LIKELY TO END BADLY.

THE SAFEST PLACES TO STRIKE ON THE BODY ARE THOSE WELL PADDED WITH MUSCLE. THE LESS MUSCLE THERE IS, THE SOFTER YOUR IMPACTS MUST BE. IN GENERAL, I'D ADVISE THAT YOU STEER CLEAR OF THE DARK AREAS IN THESE DRAWINGS, WHERE ORGANS, NERVES OR BONES HAVE VERY LITTLE PROTECTION.*

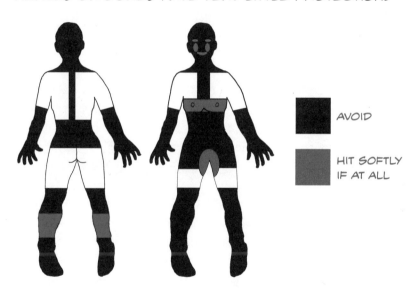

AVOID

HIT SOFTLY IF AT ALL

* YOU MAY HAVE SEEN PEOPLE STRIKE THESE PLACES IN PORN OR EROTICA. IF YOU'D LIKE TO LEARN HOW TO DO THAT, SEE THE END OF THIS CHAPTER FOR BOOKS, OR BETTER YET TAKE SOME CLASSES FROM EXPERTS AT YOUR LOCAL BDSM GROUP.

ON MARKS AND OTHER INJURIES

IT'S IMPOSSIBLE TO PREDICT WHETHER ANY GIVEN PERSON'S SKIN WILL SHOW WELTS OR BRUISES AFTER ANY PARTICULAR FORM OF PLAY – IT DEPENDS ON THEIR LEVEL OF EXPERIENCE, THEIR SKIN TYPE, THEIR HEALTH, AND SOMETIMES EVEN THE TIME OF MONTH. YOU CAN REDUCE THE CHANCE OF MARKING BY ICING THE AREA AFTER PLAY, JUST AS YOU WOULD A MINOR SPORTS INJURY. IN FACT, FIRST AID FOR PLAY INJURIES IS PRETTY MUCH THE SAME AS FIRST AID FOR SPORTS INJURIES, SO YOU CAN READ UP ON IT WITHOUT OUTING YOURSELF TO ANYONE.

IF YOUR PARTNER IS DIABETIC OR TAKES AN ANTI-CLOTTING MEDICATION, THEY ARE FAR LIKELIER TO MARK, AND MINOR INJURIES MAY CAUSE MUCH MORE OF A PROBLEM. DISCUSS YOUR PARTNER'S HEALTH WITH THEM BEFORE YOU DO SENSATION PLAY, AND IF THEY'RE NOT SURE, HAVE THEM ASK THEIR DOCTOR. (IF THEY'RE SHY, RECREATIONAL SPORTS ARE A GOOD EXCUSE.)

YOU ALREADY OWN THE BEST IMPACT TOY THERE
IS. IT LIVES AT THE END OF YOUR ARM.

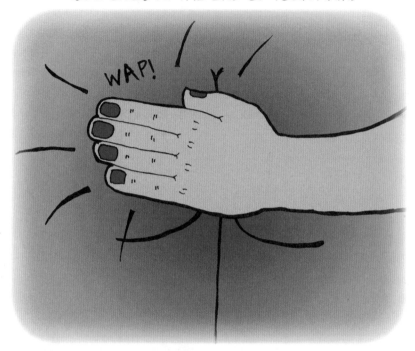

MOST RECIPIENTS FIND THE IMPACT OF A HAND MUCH
MORE AGREEABLE THAN IMPACT FROM TOYS. ALSO, A
HAND HAS A BUILT-IN FEEDBACK DEVICE: YOU'RE FEELING
WHATEVER YOUR PARTNER IS FEELING. CERTAINLY, HANDS
ARE THE BEST STARTING PLACE FOR BEGINNERS.

IT'S USEFUL TO DIVIDE IMPACT TOYS INTO TWO GROUPS: STINGY AND THUDDY. MOST BOTTOMS PREFER ONE OR THE OTHER. THAT DOESN'T MEAN YOU HAVE TO GIVE THEM ONLY THE KIND THEY LIKE (UNLESS THAT'S WHAT YOU'VE AGREED ON) - BUT KNOWING THEIR PREFERENCE ENABLES YOU TO CHALLENGE THEM WITH SOMETHING THEY DISLIKE, AND REWARD THEM WITH SOMETHING THEY LIKE.

STING COMES FROM TOYS THAT ARE RELATIVELY LIGHTWEIGHT, LIKE SWITCHES AND LEATHER OR PLASTIC PADDLES.

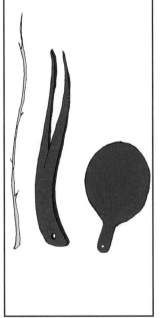

THUD COMES FROM TOYS THAT ARE HEAVY IN RELATION TO THEIR WIDTH, LIKE HEAVY PADDLES AND MANY FLOGGERS.

WITH ANY KIND OF SENSATION, BUT PARTICULARLY IMPACT, IT IS IMPORTANT TO START WITH A WARMUP. WARMUP TAKES ADVANTAGE OF HOW THE BODY NATURALLY MANAGES SENSATION – WITH ENDORPHINS, A BUILT-IN DEFENSE AGAINST PAIN. BY STARTING SLOW AND BUILDING GRADUALLY, YOU ALLOW THE ENDORPHINS TO BUILD SO THAT WHEN YOU GET TO GREATER INTENSITY, YOUR PARTNER WILL BE ABLE TO ENJOY IT.

THESE IMPACT TOYS ARE GOOD FOR BEGINNERS. ALWAYS TRY THEM, OR ANY SENSATION TOY, ON YOUR OWN SKIN FIRST. BEFORE USING ANYTHING BENDY OR FLOPPY, PRACTICE ON AN INANIMATE OBJECT SO YOU'RE SURE YOU CAN LAND THE TOY EXACTLY WHERE YOU AIM IT.

KITCHEN SPATULA

SMALL LEATHER PADDLE (I LIKE THE KIND WITH FLEECE ON THE BACK)

SOFT FLOGGER (LAMBSKIN, DEERSKIN OR LIGHT SUEDE)

SHORT RIDING CROP WITH WIDE TIP

THESE IMPACT TOYS TAKE MORE EXPERIENCE TO USE WELL.
BEFORE ACQUIRING ONE OF THESE, READ SOME OF THE
BOOKS AT THE END OF THIS CHAPTER, OR BETTER YET, LEARN
FROM SOMEONE WHO KNOWS HOW TO USE THEM SAFELY.

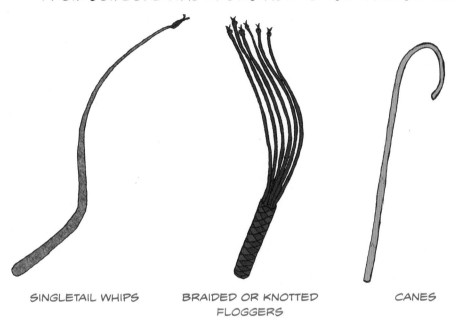

SINGLETAIL WHIPS

BRAIDED OR KNOTTED
FLOGGERS

CANES

STEER CLEAR OF ANY TOY THAT'S BEEN USED TRAUMATICALLY
OR NONCONSENSUALLY ON YOU OR YOUR PARTNER, AT LEAST
UNTIL YOU KNOW EACH OTHER VERY WELL. BE ESPECIALLY
CAREFUL WITH BELTS AND WITH FACE-SLAPPING.

ON PLAYING WITH PUNISHMENT

A LOT OF FEMALE-DOMINATION FANTASIES ARE BASED ON THE IDEA OF SOMEONE GETTING PUNISHED FOR SOMETHING – AND FOR MANY PEOPLE, THE IDEA OF PUNISHMENT IS WIRED DEEPLY INTO THEIR KINK. HOWEVER, PUNISHING SOMEONE FOR REAL-WORLD OFFENSES IS AN EMOTIONALLY RISKY FORM OF PLAY. "FUNISHMENT" – ROLEPLAY BASED ON THE IDEA OF PUNISHMENT, WITH NO REAL INTENTION TO CHANGE BEHAVIOR – IS A MUCH SAFER WAY TO EXPLORE THIS FANTASY.

IF YOU AND/OR YOUR PARTNER WANTS TO TRY ACTUAL PUNISHMENT, I STRONGLY RECOMMEND THAT YOU STICK TO RELATIVELY MINOR OFFENSES. NAIL-BITING OR LOADING THE DISHWASHER WRONG? SURE. DRINKING TOO MUCH OR BEING RUDE TO YOUR MOTHER? SAVE IT FOR THE THERAPIST'S OFFICE, NOT THE BEDROOM.

CLIPS AND CLAMPS

CLIPS AND CLAMPS ARE AN EXTREMELY VERSATILE AND AFFORDABLE WAY OF GIVING SENSATION. FROM THE HUMBLE WOODEN CLOTHESPIN TO PHANTASMAGORICAL CUSTOM CREATIONS OF STEEL AND RUBBER, THEY ALL WORK ON THE SAME PRINCIPLE: PINCHING HURTS. THEN IT GRADUALLY HURTS LESS AS THE SKIN ACCUSTOMS ITSELF TO THE SENSATION. AND THEN, WHEN THE CLAMP COMES OFF AND THE BLOOD FLOWS BACK INTO THE PINCHED SKIN, IT HURTS MOST OF ALL.

CLAMPS CAN GO PRETTY MUCH ANYWHERE YOU CAN FIND A PINCH OF SKIN, EXCEPT THE FACE. START WITH ONE OR TWO, FOR JUST A FEW MINUTES. NO MORE THAN FIFTEEN MINUTES UNTIL YOU AND YOUR PARTNER HAVE HAD SOME PRACTICE.

BE PREPARED FOR YOUR PARTNER TO JUMP, FLINCH OR YELL WHEN THE CLAMPS COME OFF.

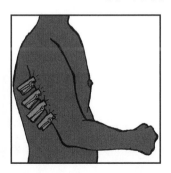 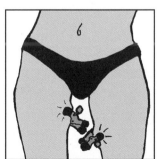 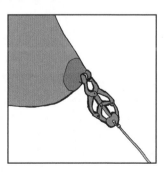

HEAT AND COLD

YOU CAN HAVE A LOT OF FUN WITH REAL OR CHEMICAL HEAT AND COLD. MOST OF THESE "TOYS" ARE ALREADY IN YOUR HOUSEHOLD, OR AVAILABLE AT YOUR LOCAL SUPERMARKET.

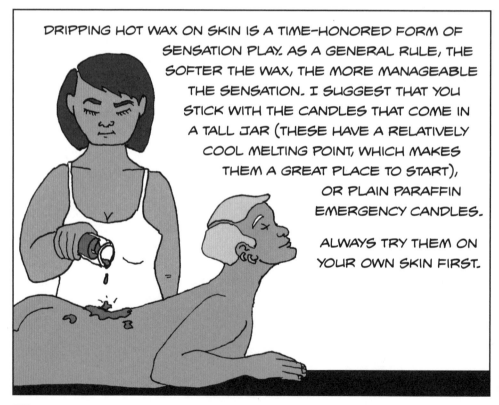

DRIPPING HOT WAX ON SKIN IS A TIME-HONORED FORM OF SENSATION PLAY. AS A GENERAL RULE, THE SOFTER THE WAX, THE MORE MANAGEABLE THE SENSATION. I SUGGEST THAT YOU STICK WITH THE CANDLES THAT COME IN A TALL JAR (THESE HAVE A RELATIVELY COOL MELTING POINT, WHICH MAKES THEM A GREAT PLACE TO START), OR PLAIN PARAFFIN EMERGENCY CANDLES.

ALWAYS TRY THEM ON YOUR OWN SKIN FIRST.

"CHEMICAL HEAT" CAN ALSO OFFER AN INTERESTING RANGE OF SENSATION. TO START WITH, TRY PUTTING A LITTLE CLOSE-UP™ TOOTH-PASTE OR CREME DE MENTHE IN YOUR HAND OR MOUTH, THEN APPLYING IT TO SENSITIVE PARTS.*

* MOST CHEMICAL HEAT IS SOLUBLE IN OIL, SO IF IT GETS TO BE TOO MUCH, COVER IT WITH SOMETHING LIKE VASELINE, BUTTER, MILK OR COLD CREAM, THEN WASH IT OFF WITH SOAP AND WATER.

TRAILING ICE OVER SKIN THAT'S BEEN REDDENED AND HEATED BY IMPACT PLAY WILL DEFINITELY GET A GASP. DO NOT INSERT ICE – THAT CAN CAUSE A DANGEROUS LOWERING OF THE HEART RATE IN SUSCEPTIBLE PEOPLE.

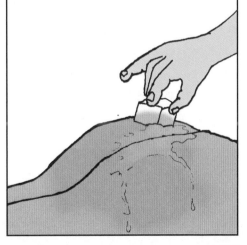

SPANKING FOR
LOVERS, BY
JANET W. HARDY
(THAT'S ME!)

FLOGGING, BY
JOSEPH BEAN

FAMILY JEWELS:
A GUIDE TO MALE
GENITAL PLAY
AND TORMENT,
BY HARDY
HABERMAN

THE TOYBAG GUIDE SERIES FROM GREENERY PRESS OFFERS CONCISE INFORMATION ON ALL KINDS OF KINK PRACTICES. HERE ARE SOME ABOUT SENSATION:

AND ONE ABOUT BASIC SAFETY AND FIRST AID INFORMATION:

THE TOYBAG GUIDE TO HOT WAX AND TEMPERATURE PLAY, BY SPECTRUM

THE TOYBAG GUIDE TO CLIPS AND CLAMPS, BY JACK RINELLA

THE TOYBAG GUIDE TO DUNGEON EMERGENCIES AND SUPPLIES, BY JAY WISEMAN

FUNDAMENTALS: CONTROL

NOT ALL KINK IS BASED ON CONTROL PLAY – OTHERWISE
KNOWN AS POWER EXCHANGE, DOMINANCE/SUBMISSION
OR D/S – BUT MUCH OF IT IS. YOUR CONTROL CAN BE
LIMITED TO ONE OR TWO ASPECTS OF YOUR PARTNER'S
BEHAVIOR, OR MANY OF THEM. IT CAN HAPPEN ONLY DURING
PRENEGOTIATED SCENES, OR CAN EXPAND OUTWARD TO
FILL MANY OR EVEN ALL OF YOUR WAKING HOURS. (FULL-
TIME CONTROL-BASED RELATIONSHIPS, DEPENDING ON
THEIR FLAVOR, MAY BE CALLED OWNER/SLAVE, DADDY
OR MOMMY/BOY OR GIRL, OR SEVERAL OTHERS. IF SUCH
RELATIONSHIPS INTEREST YOU, CHECK THE END OF THE
CHAPTER FOR SOME GOOD RESOURCES – FULL-TIME POWER
EXCHANGE IS BEYOND THE SCOPE OF THIS BOOK.)

IN THE BEGINNING, I STRONGLY RECOMMEND THAT YOU
START WITH SCENE PLAY ONLY, AND STICK TO ONE OR
TWO ASPECTS OF CONTROL. YOU CAN ADD MORE TIME
AND/OR MORE ASPECTS AS YOU AND YOUR PARTNER
LEARN MORE ABOUT EACH OTHER AND YOUR KINKS.

MOST PEOPLE RAISED AS WOMEN HAVE BEEN TAUGHT NOT TO BE BOSSY OR PUSHY, WHICH CAN MAKE IT DIFFICULT TO ACCESS YOUR "INNER DOMINANT."

THIS MAY HELP: PICTURE A PERSON WHO PROJECTS A LOT OF POWER. THEY CAN BE PEOPLE YOU'VE KNOWN, LIKE RELATIVES, TEACHERS OR BOSSES. OR THEY CAN BE FIGURES FROM BOOKS, MOVIES OR TELEVISION.

THAT'S YOUR "INNER DOMINANT." YOU CAN PRETEND TO BE THEM, OR JUST ASK THEM FOR GUIDANCE WHEN YOU'RE HAVING TROUBLE EXPRESSING DOMINANCE.

THE TRICK IS TO FIND A WAY OF DOMINATING THEM THAT SATISFIES YOUR DESIRES, WHILE MEETING THEIR CORE NEEDS. ONE OF THEIR CORE NEEDS MIGHT BE TO BE PUSHED *A LITTLE FURTHER* THAN THEY THINK THEY CAN GO, SO THEY CAN FEEL POWERFUL AND TRIUMPHANT AFTERWARD.

FINDING A BALANCE

MANY NOVICE DOMINANTS BELIEVE THAT BECAUSE THEY'RE IN CHARGE, WHAT THE SUBMISSIVE WANTS DOESN'T MATTER. IT'S A LOT MORE COMPLICATED THAN THAT.

IF YOU'RE ONLY PURSUING YOUR OWN DESIRES, YOUR PARTNER MAY GET BORED, ANGRY OR TURNED OFF. IF YOU'RE ONLY PURSUING THEIRS, WELL, THAT'S NOT REALLY DOMINANCE, IS IT?

THE HEART OF DOMINANCE (SEE P. 77) SAYS, "THE WORK OF DOMINANCE IS TO ENABLE OR INSPIRE SUBMISSION." THAT DEFINITION CLARIFIES THE BALANCE YOU SEEK BETWEEN YOUR DESIRES AND THEIRS: YOUR JOB IS TO HELP THEM DO THEIR JOB, WHICH IS TO SUBMIT TO YOU.

ON THE OTHER HAND, SOME COUPLES FIND THAT WHAT WORKS BEST FOR THEM IS FOR THE SUBMISSIVE TO ASK FOR EXACTLY WHAT THEY WANT, AND THE DOMINANT TO PROVIDE IT. THIS ISN'T EXACTLY CLASSICAL D/S, BUT IF IT WORKS FOR YOU, NOBODY GETS TO ARGUE WITH THAT.

SERVICE

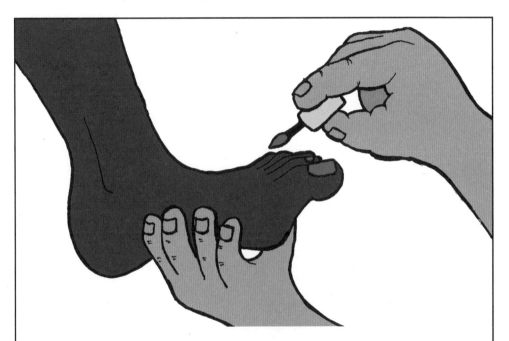

ONE FORM OF D/S THAT WORKS FOR MANY PRACTITIONERS IS FOR THE SUBMISSIVE TO PROVIDE SOME FORM OF SERVICE TO THE DOMINANT. THIS CAN BE DOMESTIC SERVICE, CLERICAL SERVICE, PERSONAL SERVICE (MASSAGES, PEDICURES, ETC.), SEXUAL SERVICE, AND/OR ANY OTHER FORM OF SERVICE THAT THEY LIKE GIVING AND YOU LIKE RECEIVING.

IF YOU ASK YOUR SERVICE-SUBMISSIVE PARTNER WHAT THEY NEED OUT OF THE SCENE, YOU MAY HEAR AN ANSWER LIKE, "I ONLY WANT TO PLEASE YOU, MISTRESS."

BY ITSELF, THAT'S NOT VERY HELPFUL (PERHAPS WHAT WOULD PLEASE YOU AT THE MOMENT IS A COUPLE OF HOURS OF TV-WATCHING, AND THAT'S PROBABLY NOT WHAT THEY'RE ASKING FOR).

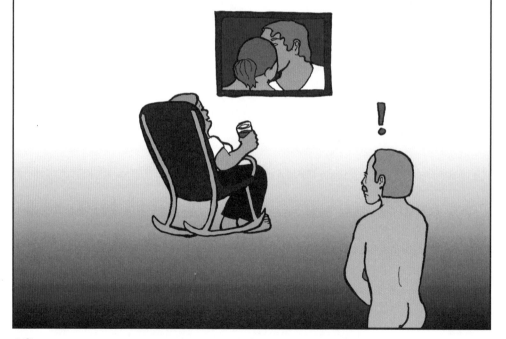

TRY ASKING THEM, "HOW WILL YOU KNOW
THAT YOU'RE PLEASING ME?"

SOME MIGHT WANT TO HEAR COMPLIMENTS ABOUT
HOW WELL THEY'RE PERFORMING THEIR SERVICE.
OTHERS, ON THE OTHER HAND, WANT TO BE TOLD HOW
INADEQUATE THEY ARE (AS LONG AS THEY KNOW DEEP
INSIDE THAT THEY REALLY AREN'T INADEQUATE). SOME
MAY MEAN THAT THEY WANT TO GIVE YOU AN ORGASM.

GIVING THEM THE "WRONG" KIND OF FEEDBACK IS A
SURE-FIRE RECIPE FOR A SCENE GONE SOUR.

SOME THOUGHTS ABOUT COLLARS

THE MOST UNIVERSALLY RECOGNIZED SYMBOL OF A CONTROL-BASED RELATIONSHIP IS THE COLLAR. KINK AND SEX BOUTIQUES OFFER COLLARS RANGING FROM DELICATE LACE CHOKERS TO CUSTOM-MADE STEEL CIRCLETS, BUT AN INEXPENSIVE DOG COLLAR FROM THE PET STORE WILL DO FINE UNTIL YOU KNOW FOR SURE THAT A COLLAR WILL BE AN ONGOING PART OF YOUR PLAY.

A COLLAR HAS A DUAL PURPOSE: ONE, TO SIGNAL TO ONLOOKERS THAT THE WEARER IS CHOOSING TO SUBMIT TO SOMEONE; TWO, AS A SYMBOL OF WHEN ITS WEARER AND THEIR PARTNER ARE IN ROLE. MANY DOMINANTS BEGIN THEIR SCENES BY PUTTING THE SUBMISSIVE'S COLLAR ON, AND END BY REMOVING IT, AS A SIGNAL THAT THE TWO PARTNERS ARE RETURNING TO AN EQUAL FOOTING.

IF A COLLAR DOESN'T WORK FOR THE FLAVOR OF YOUR SCENE OR RELATIONSHIP, ANY WEARABLE ITEM WILL DO – A RING, SOME PANTIES, A CHASTITY BELT (SEE P. 90), EVEN A SPECIAL NECKTIE. SUCH THINGS MIGHT NOT SIGNAL YOUR RELATIONSHIP TO OUTSIDERS, BUT THEY WILL TO YOU, AND THAT'S WHAT MATTERS MOST.

OBJECTIFICATION

ANOTHER FORM OF D/S IS PRETENDING THAT YOUR PARTNER IS AN OBJECT: A FOOTSTOOL, A RUG, A CHAIR. THE TRICK TO THIS ONE IS TREATING THEM AS AN OBJECT WHILE MAKING SURE THEY ARE PHYSICALLY AND EMOTIONALLY SAFE.

HUMAN PETS

MANY SUBMISSIVES ENJOY PLAYING AS ANIMALS, OFTEN PONIES, PUPPIES AND/OR KITTIES. FOR THE SUB, THE PLEASURE OFTEN COMES IN LETTING GO OF INTELLECT, FALLING INTO A PLEASANT, UNTHINKING ALTERED STATE OF CONSCIOUSNESS.

SPOT

AGE PLAY

AGE PLAY IS ANY KIND OF SCENE IN WHICH ONE OR BOTH OF YOU ARE PLAYING AS OLDER OR, MORE OFTEN, YOUNGER THAN YOU ACTUALLY ARE. SUBMISSIVES OFTEN WANT TO PLAY AS BABIES (PACIFIERS AND LOTS OF PAMPERING – DIAPERS OPTIONAL), KIDS (TOYS, ART SUPPLIES, CARTOONS), OR TEENAGERS (REBELLIOUSNESS AND SEXUAL EXPERIMENTATION).

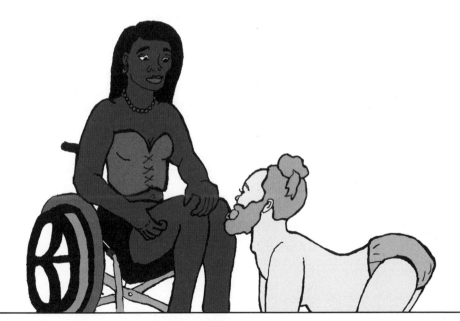

THERE'S NO LAW SAYING THAT ONLY THE SUB GETS TO AGEPLAY. HOW ABOUT IF YOU'RE THE NASTY TEENAGED BABYSITTER TO THEIR MISCHIEVOUS KID?

IT'S IMPORTANT TO REMEMBER THAT IN SOME WAYS, AN AGEPLAYER IS AS VULNERABLE AS THEY WOULD BE IF THEY WERE A REAL KID. I DON'T RECOMMEND SEXUAL AGEPLAY UNLESS YOU KNOW YOUR PARTNER VERY WELL AND YOU HAVE DONE A NUMBER OF LESS RISKY SCENES WITH THEM.

THIS FORM OF PLAY HAS TO DO WITH YOUR PARTNER PRETENDING TO BE AN UNWILLING CAPTIVE. SOME SUBS FIND THIS PLAYSTYLE PSYCHOLOGICALLY EASIER, BECAUSE THEY CAN SUBMIT WITHOUT HAVING TO FEEL "SMALL" OR WEAK.

IT'S ESPECIALLY IMPORTANT, IN ANY SCENE THAT INVOLVES PLAYING WITH UNWILLINGNESS OR RESISTANCE, FOR YOU TO HAVE A SAFEWORD THAT YOU CAN USE IF THEY START TO RESIST A LITTLE HARDER THAN YOU'RE COMFORTABLE WITH.

REMEMBER: SAFEWORDS ARE NOT JUST FOR THE SUBMITTING PARTNER. YOU NEED THEM TOO.

IF YOU WANT TO GO FURTHER...

CLEO DUBOIS AND HER HIGHLY EXPERIENCED COLLEAGUES RUN WEEKEND INTENSIVES FOR DOMINANTS AND SUBMISSIVES. CHECK OUT *CLEODUBOIS.COM.*

THE HEART OF DOMINANCE, BY ANTON FULMEN, IS MY FAVORITE BOOK ABOUT D/S OF ALL FLAVORS – SENSIBLE AND REALISTIC FOR PLAYERS OF ANY GENDER OR ORIENTATION.

FOR SERVICE-ORIENTED SCENES AND RELATIONSHIPS, *EROTIC SLAVEHOOD,* BY CHRISTINA ABERNATHY, IS A CLASSIC.

FUNDAMENTALS: SEX

OF COURSE, BEING A DOMINANT WOMAN DOESN'T NECESSARILY INVOLVE ANYONE'S SEXUAL BITS – BUT MANY PEOPLE PREFER SEX AND KINK AS A PACKAGE DEAL.

ONE OF THE ISSUES YOU'LL HAVE TO CONTEND
WITH IS OUR BROADLY HELD CULTURAL VALUE THAT
BEING DOMINANT = BEING THE PENETRATOR.

THIS BELIEF IS,
OF COURSE,
ABSURD. BUT
WHEN WE DO
DOMINANCE,
WE'RE WORKING
IN THE REALM
OF STEREOTYPE
AND ARCHETYPE
- SO YOU'LL
NEED TO FIGURE
OUT A WAY TO
PLAY WITH IT.
FORTUNATELY,
ANY SEX ACT
CAN BE DONE
EITHER BY A
DOMINANT OR A
SUBMISSIVE.

CUNNILINGUS*

THE GO-TO ACTIVITY FOR MANY FEMALE-DOMINANT PARTNERSHIPS IS, OF COURSE, CUNNILINGUS. CUNNILINGUS IS FUN AND FITS WELL INTO ALMOST ALL FEMDOM REPERTOIRES. YOU CAN MAKE YOUR PARTNER EARN THEIR ORGASM BY GIVING YOU ONE. OR THREE. OR SEVEN....

* THROUGHOUT THIS CHAPTER, I'M GOING TO ASSUME THAT YOU AND YOUR PARTNER(S) HAVE MADE INFORMED DECISIONS ABOUT WHICH SEX ACTS REQUIRE BARRIERS AND OTHER SAFER-SEX PRACTICES, AND WHICH DON'T. IF YOU NEED MORE DATA TO HELP YOU DECIDE, WWW.CDC.GOV/STD HAS UP-TO-DATE INFORMATION.

FELLATIO

THERE ARE WAYS TO PRACTICE DOMINANT FELLATIO, TOO. REMEMBER: FELLATIO INVOLVES PUTTING YOUR VERY SHARP TEETH AROUND VERY SENSITIVE PARTS.

ABOUT EDGING

"EDGING" IS A FAIRLY RECENT WORD FOR A VERY ANCIENT PRACTICE: BRINGING YOUR PARTNER TO THE EDGE OF ORGASM, THEN REDUCING THE STIMULUS TO WHERE THEY CAN'T QUITE TOPPLE OVER - AGAIN AND AGAIN, UNTIL YOU HAVE MERCY ON THEM. (THIS WORKS BEST ON PEOPLE WITH PENISES; VULVA ORGASMS FUNCTION DIFFERENTLY.)

YOU'LL ALMOST CERTAINLY NEED TO HAVE THEM IN SECURE BONDAGE TO DO THIS, AND YOU'LL NEED TO KNOW THEIR ORGASMIC PATTERN PRETTY WELL. WHAT ARE THEIR "TELLS," THE VOICE OR BODY SIGNALS THAT LET YOU KNOW THEY'RE ABOUT TO COME? USE YOUR HAND OR MOUTH OR A TOY TO GET THEM RIGHT UP TO THE "TELL" - THEN STOP AND DO SOMETHING ELSE TO THEM FOR A FEW MINUTES. NEXT TIME, PUSH THEM A LITTLE FURTHER. LATHER, RINSE, REPEAT.

WHEN YOU DECIDE THEY'VE HAD ENOUGH, OR WHEN THEY SAFEWORD, KEEP THE STIMULATION GOING UNTIL THEY FINALLY HAVE AN ORGASM. THIS MIGHT ACTUALLY BE PAINFUL AFTER SO MANY NEAR MISSES, SO TREAT THEM THE WAY YOU WOULD AFTER A PAIN SCENE, WITH PLENTY OF NURTURING AFTERCARE.

EDGING REQUIRES YOUR BEST OBSERVATIONAL AND SEXUAL SKILLS, BUT IT'S TOTALLY WORTH IT.

INTERCOURSE

DOMINANT INTERCOURSE FOR A VAGINA OWNER REQUIRES A BIT OF CREATIVITY, BUT IT CAN DEFINITELY BE DONE. WHAT POSITIONS MIGHT WORK WITH YOUR PARTNER IN BONDAGE? THINK ABOUT THEM STANDING AT THE EDGE OF THE BED WITH THEIR HANDS TIED, AS YOU LIE BACK WITH YOUR FEET BRACED AGAINST THEIR CHEST. OR PUT THEM ON THEIR BACK, WELL TIED, WHILE YOU RIDE THEM. OR ORDER THEM TO FUCK YOU WITHOUT COMING THEMSELVES.

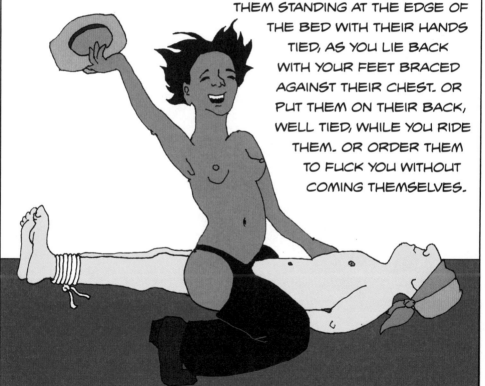

ANAL

IF YOU FEEL LIKE BEING THE PENETRATOR TONIGHT, THAT'S FUN TOO. USE ONLY ITEMS THAT WIDEN AT THE BOTTOM TO PREVENT THEIR GETTING LOST. YOU CAN USE A HARNESS AND DILDO TO HAVE YOUR OWN DICK (SEE FOLLOWING PAGE), OR YOU CAN USE YOUR FINGERS OR A PLUG. YOU'LL WANT A TOWEL OR DISPOSABLE UNDERPAD COVERING YOUR PLAY AREA.

NO SURPRISES! FOR ANY KIND OF ANAL PLAY, ESPECIALLY WITH A BEGINNER, RELAXATION IS CRITICAL. MAKE SURE THEY'RE WARM AND COMFORTABLE, AND BEGIN BY MASSAGING THE WHOLE AREA AROUND THEIR ANUS, IN A SOOTHING AND GENTLE WAY. THEN TRY JUST PRESSING IN WITH THE TIP OF YOUR INDEX FINGER.*

* IF YOUR NAILS AREN'T SHORT AND SMOOTH, PUT COTTON BALLS IN THE FINGERS OF A LATEX OR NITRILE GLOVE TO MAKE SURE NOBODY GETS HURT.

STRAP-ONS AND PEGGING

IF YOU'VE NEVER TRIED WEARING AN ADD-ON DICK TO PENETRATE A PARTNER, YOU OWE IT TO YOURSELF. MANY WOMEN FIND IT THE GATEWAY TO A BOLD NEW PERSONA.

HARNESSES COME IN VARIOUS SHAPES AND MATERIALS. YOU WANT SOMETHING THAT FITS YOU SNUGLY BUT COMFORTABLY, AND THAT HAS A STURDY O-RING TO HOLD THE DILDO IN PLACE. IF MONEY IS A CONSIDERATION, I SUGGEST STARTING WITH AN INEXPENSIVE MODEL MADE FROM SYNTHETIC FABRIC, AND GOING FOR A PRICIER ONE AFTER YOU KNOW MORE ABOUT WHAT FEELS GOOD ON YOUR BODY. (IF YOU'RE *REALLY* BROKE, TRY WHAT LESBIANS USED FOR YEARS: SNUG BUTTON-FRONT JEANS WITH THE MIDDLE COUPLE OF BUTTONS OPEN TO ACCOMMODATE YOUR DICK.)

IF YOU'RE PENETRATING ANALLY, YOU'LL NEED TIME AND LUBE – TIME TO STRETCH THEM GRADUALLY, ONE FINGER AT A TIME, UNTIL THEY CAN TAKE THREE FINGERS, PLUS MORE LUBE THAN YOU EVER THOUGHT YOU'D NEED (THERE'S ALMOST NO SUCH THING AS TOO MUCH LUBE). VAGINAL PENETRATION WORKS BEST WITH SOME LUBE AND LOTS OF FOREPLAY.

BE SURE TO SLIP A CONDOM OVER THE DILDO – THE DILDO DOESN'T MIND AND IT MAKES CLEANUP A LOT EASIER.

IF YOUR PARTNER IS NEW TO BEING ANALLY PENETRATED, START *SMALL* AND GO SLOW – MAYBE JUST ONE FINGER AT FIRST. AND FOR HEAVEN'S SAKE USE *LOTS* OF LUBE. IF YOUR PARTNER HAS A PROSTATE*, YOU'LL FIND IT ON THE FRONT WALL OF THE RECTUM A FEW INCHES IN – IT FEELS LIKE A SOFT WALNUT. ASK THEM TO TELL YOU

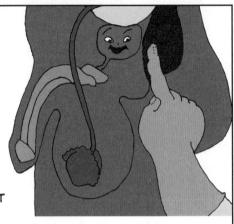

WHEN YOU'VE FOUND IT, AND FOLLOW THEIR LEAD ABOUT HOW MUCH PRESSURE FEELS GOOD.

DON'T BUY LUBE THAT NUMBS – THOSE SENSATIONS ARE THERE TO TELL YOU THAT SOMETHING'S NOT RIGHT. MANY PEOPLE PREFER SILICONE LUBE FOR ANAL PLAY.

IF THEY SAY SOMETHING IS HURTING, SLOW DOWN AND ADD MORE LUBE. ONCE THEY CAN EASILY TAKE THREE OF YOUR FINGERS, YOU CAN EASE THE TOY IN, WITH PLENTY OF ATTENTION TO BODY LANGUAGE. REMEMBER TO APPLY MORE LUBE OFTEN, BOTH TO THE TOY/FINGERS AND TO THE ANUS.

* A SMALL GLAND THAT PRODUCES THE FLUID IN WHICH SPERM SWIM. MOST BUT NOT ALL PROSTATE OWNERS FIND PRESSURE THERE SEXY.

CHASTITY

EVERY DOMME AGREES: IT'S MUCH EASIER TO GET A HORNY PERSON INTO A SUBMISSIVE MINDSET. THUS, IT'S TO OUR ADVANTAGE TO KEEP OUR PARTNERS AS HORNY AS POSSIBLE.

TAKING CONTROL OF THEIR ORGASMS CAN MAKE THAT HAPPEN. YOU CAN ACCOMPLISH THAT WITH A VERBAL AGREEMENT (IF YOU TRUST THEM TO TELL THE TRUTH), OR YOU CAN BUY OR MAKE A CHASTITY DEVICE TO WHICH YOU HOLD THE KEY. IF YOU GET DEEPER INTO CHASTITY, YOU CAN TRY "EDGING" (P. 82) WITHOUT THE ORGASMIC REWARD AT THE END. YOU'LL BE AMAZED HOW COOPERATIVE YOUR PARTNER BECOMES WHEN THEY'RE DEPENDENT ON YOU TO GET OFF!

ENERGY SEX

MANY PEOPLE HAVE LEARNED TO FEEL ORGASMIC ENERGY THROUGHOUT THEIR WHOLE BODIES, RATHER THAN JUST IN THEIR GENITALS. TECHNIQUES FOR GETTING THERE INCLUDE BREATHING, UNDULATING THE HIPS, RHYTHMICALLY TIGHTENING THE PELVIC MUSCLES, AND GAZING INTO A PARTNER'S EYES.

MOST CITIES HAVE TANTRA INSTRUCTORS WHO SPECIALIZE IN HELPING PEOPLE LEARN THESE TECHNIQUES. HOWEVER, A LOT OF TANTRA CLASSES ARE NOT ACCEPTING OF FEMALE-DOMINANT ENERGY, SO DO SOME HOMEWORK BEFORE YOU SIGN UP FOR ANYTHING. YOU CAN BUY GOOD, GENDER-AFFIRMING, KINK-POSITIVE BOOKS ABOUT ENERGY SEX.

88

IF YOU WANT TO GO FURTHER...

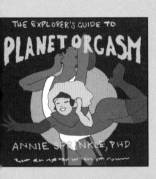  

ANNIE SPRINKLE'S EXPLORER'S GUIDE TO PLANET ORGASM OFFERS INSIGHTS AND INSTRUCTIONS FOR ALL KINDS OF ORGASMS, INCLUDING ENERGY ORGASMS.

URBAN TANTRA, BY BARBARA CARRELLAS, TEACHES TANTRA TECHNIQUES FOR PEOPLE OF ALL GENDERS AND ORIENTATIONS. BARBARA AND HER COLLEAGUES ALSO TEACH URBAN TANTRA WORKSHOPS.

THE TOYBAG GUIDE TO CHASTITY PLAY, BY MISTRESS SIMONE, A LONGTIME LIFESTYLE DOMINANT, IS A HANDY GUIDE TO CONTROLLING YOUR PARTNER'S ORGASMS.

FUNDAMENTALS: FETISH

MANY PEOPLE BELIEVE THAT HAVING A FETISH MEANS THE FETISHIST IS UNABLE TO GET TURNED ON WITHOUT THE PRESENCE OF THE FETISH OBJECT. IN MY EXPERIENCE, THIS IS RARELY TRUE: THE FETISH IS THE CHOCOLATE SAUCE THAT TURNS PLAIN ICE CREAM INTO A YUMMY SUNDAE.

THE COMMONEST FETISH IN KINK-LAND IS LEATHER, WITH RUBBER A CLOSE SECOND.

LEATHER IS PRETTY EASY TO BUILD INTO YOUR EVERYDAY WARDROBE IF YOU HAVE THE CASH (IF NOT, HAUNT YOUR LOCAL THRIFT STORES). RUBBER OR LATEX MAY GET YOU STARED AT, BUT MAYBE YOU'LL LIKE THAT.

OTHER COMMON CLOTHING FETISHES INCLUDE LINGERIE, CORSETS, STOCKINGS, SPANDEX AND FUR.

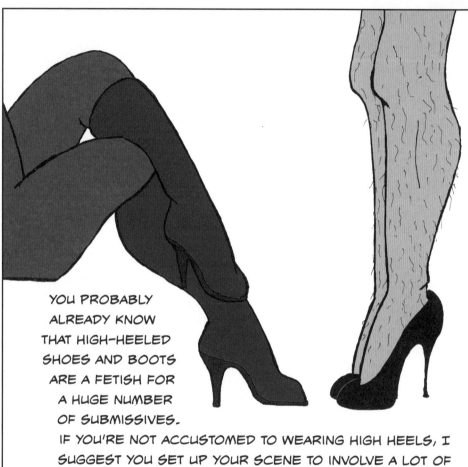

YOU PROBABLY ALREADY KNOW THAT HIGH-HEELED SHOES AND BOOTS ARE A FETISH FOR A HUGE NUMBER OF SUBMISSIVES.

IF YOU'RE NOT ACCUSTOMED TO WEARING HIGH HEELS, I SUGGEST YOU SET UP YOUR SCENE TO INVOLVE A LOT OF SITTING ON YOUR PART. OR MAKE *THEM* WEAR THE HEELS.

CROSSDRESSING AND "FORCED FEMINIZATION"

THE DESIRE TO BE "MADE" TO CROSSDRESS IS SO COMMON THAT MANY PROFESSIONAL DOMINATRIXES MAINTAIN SPECIAL ROOMS FULL OF WIGS, PLUS-SIZED HEELS AND LINGERIE.

THE DESIRE BEHIND THIS KINK SEEMS TO BE A MIXTURE OF HUMILIATION AND SAFETY. BEING MADE TO BE "FEMININE" IS ON ONE HAND A REDUCTION IN STATUS*, AND ON THE OTHER AN ESCAPE FROM THE DEMANDS OUR CULTURE STILL PLACES ON MEN TO BE STRONG, STOIC AND EMOTIONALLY CLOSED OFF.

IT'S ALSO WORTH REMEMBERING THAT FEW PEOPLE WHO GROW UP MALE EVER GET THE CHANCE TO BE THE OBJECTS OF VISUAL LUST. THE ONLY OUTLET MANY HAVE FOR THEIR DESIRE TO LOOK SEXY IS TO WEAR THE CLOTHES OF A DIFFERENT GENDER.

HAVING THIS KINK DOESN'T NECESSARILY MEAN THAT THEY'RE TRANS. IT DOESN'T NECESSARILY MEAN THAT THEY AREN'T, EITHER.

FEMINIZATION HAS MANY OF THE SAME VULNERABILITIES AS AGE PLAY (SEE P. 77). TREAT YOUR NEW "GIRLFRIEND" WITH CARE.

* FEW IF ANY FORCED-FEMINIZATION KINKSTERS ACTUALLY BELIEVE WOMEN TO BE OF LOWER STATUS. REMEMBER, WHEN WE DO KINK, WE'RE PLAYING IN THE REALM OF STEREOTYPE AND ARCHETYPE, NOT REALITY.

SOME FOLKS FETISHIZE PARTICULAR BODY FLUIDS, OFTEN URINE OR MENSTRUAL BLOOD. FETISHIZING CERTAIN ACTIVITIES, SUCH AS SMOKING, IS ALSO COMMON.

A FETISH FOR A PARTICULAR BODY PART IS TECHNICALLY CALLED A "PARTIALISM." DESIRE FOR FEET, BUTTOCKS, HAIR AND ARMPITS ARE COMMON PARTIALISMS.

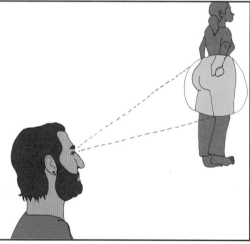

SOME SUBMISSIVES WILL WANT TO "WORSHIP" PARTS OF YOU AND/OR YOUR OUTFIT. THAT MEANS THAT THEY WILL DEVOTE THEMSELVES TO IT BY LICKING IT, KISSING IT, BATHING IT, POLISHING IT, CARESSING IT, ETC.

IF THEY'RE SMART, THEY'LL MAKE SURE *YOU* DON'T FEEL LEFT OUT OF THIS PROCESS. MANY DOMMES COMPLAIN OF SUBS WHO GET SO FOCUSED ON WORSHIPING FEET, FOR EXAMPLE, THAT THEY FORGET A WOMAN EXISTS ABOVE THE KNEES. A BODY WORSHIP SESSION SHOULD FEEL GOOD TO YOU TOO.

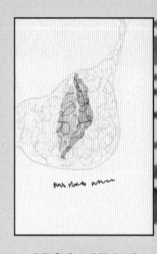

FETISH: FASHION, SEX & POWER, BY VALERIE STEELE – A THOROUGH OVERVIEW OF FETISHES AND THEIR HISTORIES.

THE TOYBAG GUIDE TO FOOT AND SHOE WORSHIP, BY MIDORI – EVERYTHING YOU NEED FOR PLEASURE BELOW THE ANKLES.

DESIGN BEHIND DESIRE: THE SENSUOUS TEXTURES OF WANTING, BY LISA Z. MORGAN, IS A STUNNING COFFEE-TABLE TRIBUTE TO FETISH.

PUTTING IT ALL TOGETHER

NOW THAT YOU'VE LEARNED THE BASICS, IT'S TIME TO BEGIN ASSEMBLING THEM INTO A START-TO-FINISH SCENE. I'LL SUGGEST SOME POSSIBLE SCENARIOS TO GET YOU STARTED IN THE NEXT CHAPTER.

THE FIRST THING YOU AND YOUR PARTNER NEED TO DO IS DISCUSS WHAT EACH OF YOU WANTS OUT OF YOUR SCENE.

- WHAT ACTIVITIES, FEELINGS, FETISHES, ETC., DOES EACH OF YOU NEED FOR THE SCENE TO FEEL COMPLETE?

- ARE THERE ANY CONFLICTS (PARTNER A WANTS SOMETHING THAT PARTNER B DOESN'T FEEL EXCITED ABOUT DOING)? IF SO, WHAT COMPROMISES MIGHT WORK?

- HOW WILL YOU LET EACH OTHER KNOW IF YOU NEED TO STOP?

- WHAT PRECAUTIONS DO YOU NEED TO TAKE AGAINST EMERGENCIES, UNPLANNED INTERRUPTIONS, FREAKOUTS?

- THIS IS ALSO A GOOD TIME TO ARRANGE TO TALK TO EACH OTHER THE NEXT DAY TO DISCUSS HOW THINGS WENT. IDEALLY, THIS SHOULD BE A FACE-TO-FACE MEETING, BUT PHONE OR EMAIL WILL DO IN A PINCH.

BEGINNING YOUR SCENE

I SUGGEST STARTING YOUR SCENE WITH A FEW MINUTES OF PERSONAL CONNECTION. IF YOU'RE USING A SYMBOL LIKE A COLLAR, PUT IT ON YOUR PARTNER AS PART OF A SOLEMN RITUAL. IF NOT, CONNECT WITH ONE ANOTHER THROUGH PHYSICAL TOUCH, EYE-GAZING, BREATHING TOGETHER, OR WHATEVER OTHER STRUCTURE PULLS YOU OUT OF THE OUTSIDE WORLD AND INTO THE PROTECTED WORLD OF YOUR SCENE.

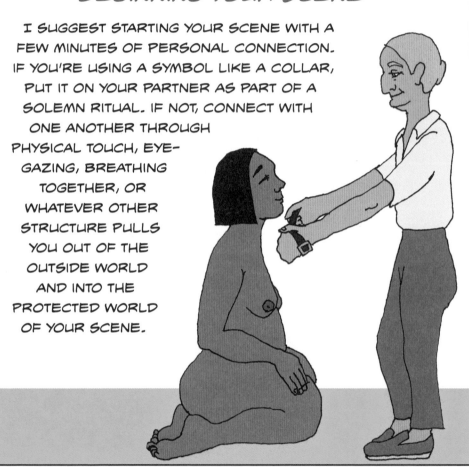

HAVING TROUBLE FEELING YOUR DOMINANCE? SOME FOLKS HAVE A PARTICULAR ACTIVITY THAT ALWAYS MAKES THEM FEEL DOMINANT. FOR EXAMPLE, IF YOUR SCENE INCLUDES SEX, HAVING YOUR PARTNER DO SOMETHING TO AROUSE YOU CAN HELP YOU GET INTO THE RIGHT HEADSPACE.

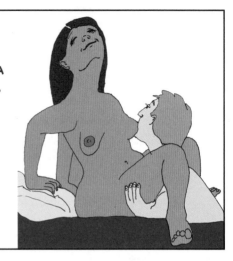

DURING THE SCENE, IF YOU GET STUCK ABOUT WHAT TO DO NEXT - SOME PEOPLE CALL THIS BLANK-PAPERITIS - JUST STOP. TAKE A MOMENT TO FIND YOUR BREATH AND BE STILL. TOUCH YOUR PARTNER IF THAT FEELS RIGHT. THE NEXT THING TO DO WILL NEARLY ALWAYS COME TO YOU.

PACE YOURSELF: TIME GOES FASTER INSIDE THE ROPES THAN OUTSIDE, AND WAITING CAN BE DELICIOUS.

MANY DOMMES FIND WHAT WORKS BEST IS FOR INTENSITY TO COME IN WAVES: YOU CHALLENGE THEM WITH SOMETHING DIFFICULT, THEN BACK OFF, THEN RAMP THINGS UP A BIT HIGHER, THEN BACK OFF AGAIN. PLAN YOUR SCENE SO THE END COMES AFTER PEAK INTENSITY: A CERTAIN NUMBER OF STROKES, A PARTICULARLY DIFFICULT TASK, ETC. MANY SUBS FIND IT EASIER TO MANAGE THAT PEAK IF THEY KNOW IT SIGNALS THE END OF THE SCENE.

THE PERIOD AFTER THE SCENE IS FOR AFTERCARE, WHEN YOU AND YOUR PARTNER CARE FOR ONE ANOTHER AND PROVIDE NURTURANCE. CUDDLING IS AWESOME FOR THIS, AS IS FEEDING EACH OTHER - INTENSE PLAY CAN DEHYDRATE AND REDUCE BLOOD SUGAR, SO HAVE DRINKS AND SNACKS ON HAND.

DON'T SKIMP ON AFTERCARE - MANY PLAYERS FIND IT THE MOST REWARDING PART OF THE SCENE. (A FEW SUBS DON'T WANT IT AT ALL. TALK ABOUT THIS DURING YOUR NEGOTIATION.)

NEITHER OF YOU SHOULD TRY TO DRIVE A CAR, OR DO ANY OTHER COMPLEX TASK, FOR AN HOUR OR TWO. WHETHER IT FEELS THAT WAY OR NOT, YOU'RE BOTH STILL IN AN ALTERED STATE. RELAX AND ENJOY IT.

SCENES TO GET YOU STARTED

HERE ARE THREE SCENES THAT MIGHT BE SUITABLE TO DO AS YOUR AND YOUR PARTNER'S FIRST SCENE TOGETHER. ONE IS PRIMARILY ABOUT BONDAGE, ONE IS PRIMARILY ABOUT SENSATION, AND ONE IS PRIMARILY ABOUT CONTROL. THEY'RE NOT INTENDED AS HARD-AND-FAST SCRIPTS, BUT AS INSPIRATION TO HELP YOU CREATE A SCENE OF YOUR OWN.

THE MOST IMPORTANT THING ABOUT THIS FIRST SCENE ISN'T THAT IT SHOULD BE THE MOST PHENOMENALLY FULFILLING SCENE EVER IN THE HISTORY OF KINK. WHAT'S FAR MORE IMPORTANT IS THAT IT NOT GO BADLY – IT'S EASIER TO DO A LITTLE MORE NEXT TIME THAN IT IS TO RECOVER FROM A MISHAP.

GENERAL PRINCIPLES

– DISCUSS EVERYTHING YOU'RE ABOUT TO DO WITH YOUR PARTNER BEFOREHAND – YOU CAN READ THIS CHAPTER TOGETHER, IF YOU LIKE. GIVE THEM A CHANCE TO VOICE ANY CONCERNS OR OBJECTIONS, AND TAKE THOSE CONCERNS SERIOUSLY, REVISING YOUR PLAN AS NEEDED.

– IF SOMETHING GOES WRONG, OR JUST DOESN'T SEEM LIKE IT'S WORKING, STOP. TAKE A MOMENT TO RECONNECT WITH YOUR PARTNER. DON'T BE DISCOURAGED; THIS HAPPENS TO EVERYONE SOMETIMES. FIX THE PROBLEM, THEN DECIDE TOGETHER WHETHER TO TRY SOMETHING DIFFERENT, OR END THE SCENE THERE AND TRY ANOTHER DAY.

– RAMP UP SLOWLY. NO ZERO-TO-SIXTY STUFF.

– CHECK IN OFTEN WITH YOUR PARTNER – IT'S FINE TO ASK SOMETHING LIKE, "ARE YOU STILL WITH ME?" OR "ON A SCALE OF ONE TO TEN, HOW INTENSE IS THAT FOR YOU?" IT'S ALSO FINE TO ASK THEM WHAT INTENSITY THEY WANT, USING THE SAME ONE-TO-TEN SCALE.

– CHOOSE A SAFEWORD BECAUSE IT'S A GOOD HABIT TO GET INTO. BUT FOR AT LEAST YOUR FIRST SEVERAL SCENES, ANYTHING THAT SOUNDS LIKE RESISTANCE –

103

"NO," "PLEASE," "STOP" AND SO ON – MEANS THAT YOU SHOULD STOP AND INVESTIGATE WHAT'S GOING ON.

– DON'T TRY TOO MANY NEW THINGS AT ONCE. IF YOU DO A FIRST SESSION THAT INCLUDES TWO THINGS YOU'VE NEVER DONE BEFORE, THAT'S PLENTY. ONE IS EVEN BETTER – THAT WAY IF SOMETHING DOES GO WRONG, YOU'LL KNOW WHAT CAUSED IT.

– ALLOW PLENTY OF TIME FOR AFTERCARE, AND CHECK IN WITH EACH OTHER THE NEXT DAY TO SEE HOW YOU FEEL. BE PREPARED FOR ONE OR BOTH OF YOU TO FEEL A BIT TEARY, TIRED OR EMOTIONALLY OFF-BALANCE; THAT HAPPENS TO EVERYONE, AT LEAST SOMETIMES. TAKE CARE OF YOURSELF AND EACH OTHER WITH PLENTY OF REASSURANCE AND PHYSICAL NURTURING.

– FOR THE PURPOSES OF THIS BOOK, I'M GOING TO ASSUME THAT SEX IS A POSSIBILITY FOR THE TWO OF YOU. IF NOT, FIGURE OUT ANOTHER ACTIVITY THAT YOU CAN USE AS A REWARD – SOME TENDER TOUCHES, FEEDING THEM SOMETHING TASTY, WHATEVER.

– YOU DID IT! EVEN IF THE SCENE FELT TIMID AND BEGINNER-Y TO YOU, THAT'S GREAT – YOU CAN ALWAYS ADD A BIT MORE NEXT TIME. CONGRATULATE YOURSELF AND THEM!

A FIRST BONDAGE SCENE

TAKE A FEW MINUTES TO CONNECT WITH YOUR PARTNER. USING EYE CONTACT AND/OR SOFT TOUCH, LET GO OF OUTSIDE CONCERNS SO THAT BOTH OF YOU CAN BECOME AS PRESENT AS YOU CAN BE.

I'M GOING TO START BY EXPLAINING HOW TO MAKE A BASIC ROPE BODY HARNESS.* A HARNESS SHOULDN'T IMPEDE THEIR MOVEMENT AT ALL; SOME ROPE-LOVERS LIKE TO WEAR ONE UNDER THEIR CLOTHES ON OCCASION. THE PICTURES ON THE NEXT PAGE SHOULD GIVE YOU AN IDEA OF WHAT YOU'RE GOING FOR.

START BY DRAPING A 40' ROPE AROUND THEIR NECKS SO THE ENDS DANGLE DOWN THEIR CHESTS TO THE FLOOR.

MAKE ONE SIMPLE OVERHAND KNOT OR SQUARE KNOT WITH BOTH ROPES AT THE MIDDLE OF THEIR CHEST. MAKE A SECOND ONE AT ABOUT THEIR NAVEL. MAKE THE THIRD AT AROUND THEIR GROIN. BRING THE ENDS BETWEEN THEIR LEGS TO EITHER SIDE OF THEIR GROIN.

* FOR REASONS OF LENGTH, I CAN'T SHOW YOU STEP-BY-STEP DRAWINGS OF HOW TO DO THIS HARNESS. GIVE YOURSELF PERMISSION TO BE A BEGINNER, AND TRY NOT TO GET FRUSTRATED. IF YOU REALLY FEEL STUCK, ASK YOUR PARTNER OR A FRIEND TO WORK ON IT WITH YOU, AND/OR REFER TO ONE OR MORE OF THE BOOKS ON P. 46 AND IN THE RESOURCE GUIDE.

BRING THE ENDS UP TO THE ROPE BEHIND THEIR
NECK, AND TIE IT OFF WITH A SQUARE KNOT.

SEPARATE THE TWO ENDS AND BRING THEM UNDER YOUR
PARTNER'S ARMS TO THE FRONT. PASS EACH END AROUND
ONE OF THE ROPES BETWEEN THE FIRST TWO KNOTS.

BRING THE ENDS AROUND TO THE BACK, PULLING THE
ROPES APART INTO A DIAMOND SHAPE. CROSS THE
ENDS INTO AN X AT THEIR MIDBACK. BRING THEM BACK
TO THE FRONT, PASSING EACH END AROUND ONE OF THE
ROPES BETWEEN THE SECOND AND THIRD KNOT.

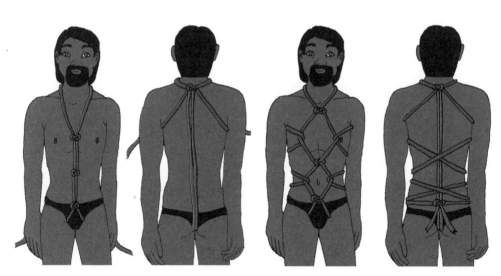

COMPLETE THE HARNESS BY BRINGING THE
ENDS BACK AROUND AND TYING THEM OFF IN A
SQUARE KNOT AT YOUR PARTNER'S BACK.

IN FUTURE SESSIONS, YOU CAN ADD MORE KNOTS AND MORE
DIAMONDS FOR A MORE COMPLEX HARNESS. YOU CAN ALSO
TIE THEIR HANDS OR FEET TO THE HARNESS, OR ATTACH IT
TO AN INANIMATE OBJECT LIKE A POST OR BEDFRAME.

GETTING THE HARNESS ON AND LOOKING GOOD MIGHT
TAKE A WHILE. ASK YOUR PARTNER TO DESCRIBE
WHAT THEY'RE FEELING. ENJOY THE JOURNEY
WITHOUT GETTING HUNG UP ON THE DESTINATION.

THAT'S PROBABLY ENOUGH FOR A FIRST SESSION – GO ON TO
AFTERCARE, AND/OR TO SEX IF THAT'S THE WAY YOU ROLL.

A FIRST SENSATION SCENE

THE MOST POPULAR FORM OF SENSATION PLAY FOR MANY PLAYERS IS SPANKING, SO THIS FIRST SCENE IS ABOUT THAT. TALK TO YOUR PARTNER FIRST ABOUT ANY HISTORY THEY MAY HAVE HAD WITH BEING SPANKED PUNITIVELY OR NONCONSENSUALLY. IF SPANKING IS A TRIGGER FOR THEM (OR YOU), TRY SOME CLAMPS (P. 57) OR WAX (P. 58) INSTEAD.

IS THIS SPANKING BECAUSE THEY'VE BEEN "BAD" OR BECAUSE THEY'VE BEEN "GOOD"? FIND OUT WHERE THEIR HEAD IS AT ON THIS QUESTION BEFORE YOU BEGIN. IT WILL AFFECT BOTH THE SPANKING ITSELF AND THE WORDS YOU SAY WHILE YOU GIVE IT.

TAKE A FEW MINUTES TO CONNECT WITH YOUR PARTNER. USING EYE CONTACT AND/OR SOFT TOUCH, LET GO OF OUTSIDE CONCERNS SO THAT BOTH OF YOU CAN BECOME AS PRESENT AS YOU CAN BE.

THEN HAVE YOUR PARTNER LIE FACE DOWN ON A BED, MASSAGE TABLE, OR A WELL-PADDED FLOOR. PUT A COUPLE OF PILLOWS UNDER THEIR HIPS IF THAT FEELS MORE COMFORTABLE.

CARESS THEIR BOTTOM GENTLY FOR A BIT. VERY
GRADUALLY, BEGIN ADDING SMALL SMACKS – HARDLY
MORE THAN LOVETAPS AT FIRST – INTO YOUR CARESSES.

BUILD GRADUALLY TO WHERE YOUR SMACKS
MAKE A SLAPPING SOUND. PAUSE AFTER EVERY
FEW SMACKS TO CARESS A BIT MORE.

WHAT MAKES IMPACT PLAY INTENSE IS LESS ABOUT
HOW HARD YOU HIT AND MORE ABOUT HOW FAST
YOU HIT. START SLOW AND BUILD GRADUALLY.

DEPENDING ON THE FLAVOR OF SPANKING YOU AGREED
ON, TELL THEM HOW WONDERFUL THEY ARE OR HOW
NAUGHTY THEY'VE BEEN. IF YOU NOTICE THEM TENSING
UP OR SEEMING UNHAPPY, SLOW DOWN AND USE SOFTER
SPANKS, AND JUST TELL THEM HOW WONDERFUL THEY ARE.

FOR THE LAST SEQUENCE OF A DOZEN SPANKS, TELL
THEM THEY GET TO CONTROL THEM. THEY WILL ASK FOR
EACH SPANK USING A NUMBER FROM ONE (HARDLY
NOTICEABLE) TO TEN (AS HARD AS YOU'RE WILLING TO HIT).
LET THEM COUNT THE SPANKS OFF FOR THEMSELVES.

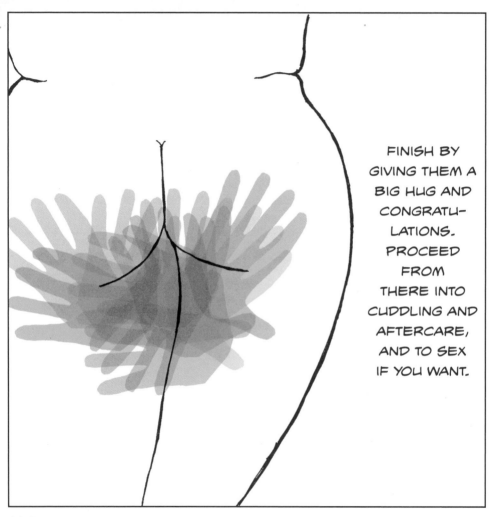

FINISH BY GIVING THEM A BIG HUG AND CONGRATU-LATIONS. PROCEED FROM THERE INTO CUDDLING AND AFTERCARE, AND TO SEX IF YOU WANT.

A FIRST CONTROL SCENE

IN THIS SCENE, YOU WON'T BE DOING ANY SENSATION OR BONDAGE AT ALL, JUST CONTROLLING THEIR MOVEMENT AND BEHAVIOR.

TAKE A FEW MINUTES TO CONNECT WITH YOUR PARTNER. USING EYE CONTACT AND/OR SOFT TOUCH, LET GO OF OUTSIDE CONCERNS SO THAT BOTH OF YOU CAN BECOME AS PRESENT AS YOU CAN BE.

THEN, INSTRUCT THEM TO KNEEL IN FRONT OF YOU. THEY MIGHT WANT A CUSHION UNDER THEIR KNEES AND/OR A ROLLED-UP TOWEL SUPPORTING THEIR ANKLES.

SPEND SOME TIME FUSSING OVER TEACHING THEM EXACTLY THE KNEELING POSITION YOU LIKE. SHOULD THEIR EYES BE UP, OR CAST DOWN AT THE FLOOR? HOW STRAIGHT SHOULD THEIR BACK BE? WHERE SHOULD THEIR HANDS BE? HOW FAR APART ARE THEIR KNEES? ARE THEIR TOES TUCKED UP UNDER THE BALLS OF THEIR FEET, OR EXTENDED BACKWARD ONTO THE FLOOR? USE YOUR PICKINESS TO EXTEND THE EXPERIENCE AS LONG AS THEIR KNEES HOLD OUT.

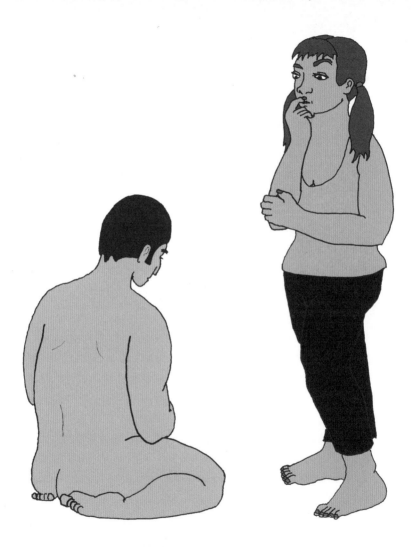

WHEN YOU'RE SATISFIED, ALLOW THEM TO BREAK POSITION
AND MOVE INTO SOMETHING MORE COMFORTABLE
LIKE SITTING. PULL UP A CHAIR IN FRONT OF THEM AND
INSTRUCT THEM TO RUB YOUR FEET. (YOU MAY WANT TO
HAVE A LITTLE MASSAGE OIL ON HAND FOR THIS.)

USE THE SAME FUSSINESS YOU USED BEFORE TO TEACH
THEM HOW TO RUB YOUR FEET EXACTLY HOW YOU LIKE. HOW
HARD OR SOFT? ANY PARTS THAT DON'T LIKE TO BE TOUCHED?
HOW DOES IT FEEL WHEN THEY PULL ON YOUR TOES?

SPEND ENOUGH TIME ON THIS THAT YOUR FEET
FEEL TERRIFIC BY THE TIME IT'S THROUGH.

LET THEM RISE UP TO A STANDING POSITION. GIVE THEM A
BIG HUG AND TELL THEM THAT THEY LEARNED A LOT ABOUT
HOW TO PLEASE YOU AND YOU'RE VERY PROUD OF THEM.

THEN MOVE ON TO WHATEVER COMES NEXT:
AFTERCARE AND/OR CUDDLING AND/OR SEX.

THANK YOU!

I HOPE YOU'VE ENJOYED READING AND LEARNING
ABOUT THE BASICS OF BEING A FEMALE DOMINANT.

BECAUSE I WROTE THIS BOOK AS AN INTRODUCTION
FOR BEGINNERS, I HAVE BEEN LIMITED IN HOW MUCH
INFORMATION I CAN PROVIDE. IF YOU THINK BDSM
IS GOING TO BE A SIGNIFICANT PART OF YOUR LIFE, I
ENCOURAGE YOU TO GO ON LEARNING – FROM BOOKS,
FROM EXPERTS, AND FROM OTHER PEOPLE LIKE YOU.

THE RESOURCE GUIDE ON THE FOLLOWING PAGES SHOULD
GIVE YOU SOME IDEAS ABOUT WHERE TO FIND MORE
INFORMATION, WHERE TO FIND FRIENDS AND MENTORS IN
THE SCENE, AND HOW TO FIND PARTNERS INTERESTED IN
THE KIND OF PLAY YOU WANT TO DO. I'VE ALSO INCLUDED
A FEW RESOURCES TO HELP YOU SOLVE PROBLEMS YOU
MAY ENCOUNTER ALONG YOUR JOURNEY AS A DOMINANT.

THANKS AGAIN FOR YOUR TIME AND ATTENTION. AND
DON'T FORGET THE MOST ESSENTIAL ADVICE OF ALL:

HAVE FUN!

RESOURCE GUIDE

Please also check the "If You Want to Go Further..." pages at the end of most chapters.

BOOKS

General kink titles

The New Bottoming Book and *The New Topping Book*, Dossie Easton and Janet W. Hardy. Greenery Press, 2001 & 2002. Guides to your physical and emotional safety and growth as you explore kink.

Playing Well With Others: Your Field Guide to Discovering, Exploring & Navigating the Kink and BDSM Communities. Lee Harrington & Mollena Williams, Greenery Press, 2012. Invaluable instructions on finding and joining the BDSM/kink communities.

Screw the Roses, Send Me the Thorns: The Romance and Sexual Sorcery of Sadomasochism, Phillip Miller & Molly Devon. Mystic Rose Books, 1995. A classic.

Tongue Tied: Untangling Communication in Sex, Kink, and Relationships, Stella Harris. Cleis Press, 2018. How to ask for what you want and communicate while you're getting it.

The Ultimate Guide to Kink: BDSM, Role Play and the Erotic Edge, Tristan Taormino. Cleis Press, 2002. Essays on the hows and whys of kink by experts nationwide.

General sexuality

Anal Pleasure and Health: A Guide for Men, Women and Couples, Jack Morin, Ph.D. Down There Press, 2010. A thorough and well-researched guide to anal pleasure.

Girl Sex 101, Alison Moon. Lunatic Ink, 2017. Comprehensive and fun-to-read info about how to have sex with women (including trans women), and as a woman.

The Guide to Getting It On: Unzipped, Paul Joannides, Ph.D. Goofy Foot Press, 2017. A terrific guide to all forms of sexual interaction, particularly useful to young adults.

The New Male Sexuality: The Truth About Men, Sex, and Pleasure, Bernie Zilbergeld, Ph.D. Bantam, 1999. How men are wired, and how women can tap into that wiring.

Sex for One: The Joy of Selfloving, Betty Dodson, Ph.D. Harmony Press, 1996. Great sex starts with great solo sex, and great solo sex for women starts with Betty Dodson.

Dealing with relationship issues

The Ethical Slut: A Practical Guide to Polyamory, Open Relationships, and Other Freedoms in Sex and Love, Janet W. Hardy and Dossie Easton. Ten Speed Press, 2017. Guidelines and ideas for exploring alternatives to traditional monogamy.

The Jealousy Workbook: Exercises and Insights for Managing Open Relationships, Kathy Labriola. Greenery Press, 2013. Jealousy can affect any relationship. This workbook provides many worksheets that you can do, solo or partnered, to learn to deal with it.

More Than Two: A Practical Guide to Ethical Polyamory, Franklin Veaux and Eve Rickett. Thorntree Press, 2014. A sensible introduction to the logistics of loving in multiples.

When Someone You Love Is Kinky, Dossie Easton and Catherine A. Liszt ("Catherine" is a pen name; she is actually me, Janet Hardy). Greenery Press, 2000. The book you can show to your partner, parent, coworker or friend to help them understand.

BLOGS AND WEBSITES

BDSM events, www.thebdsmeventspage.com/events.html. If you have any interest in attending a conference, contest or other kink get-together, check this page first to see what's coming up. If nothing sounds right, try entering "bdsm event [name of your community]" into your favorite search engine.

BDSM groups, en.wikipedia.org/wiki/List_of_BDSM_organizations, lists many of the best-established groups. If nothing sounds right, try entering "bdsm group [name of your community]" into your favorite search engine.

Erotic Awakening, featuring Dan and dawn, www.eroticawakening.com. Although Dan and dawn are in a male-dominant relationship, they interview guests and experts from all corners of the kink universe. Smart and responsible.

Fetlife (www.fetlife.com) is sometimes called "The Facebook of alt-sex," and that's a pretty good description. It has the same problems as Facebook - little control over disruptive or abusive members, many "one true way" proselytizers, and no way to determine if anyone is who they say they are. But it also has the same advantages - you can meet people who share your interests, and learn from folks who have been doing kink a lot longer than you. It's also the primary spot where people advertise upcoming events, conferences, etc. Check it out, but with many grains of salt.

Kink Academy, www.kinkacademy.com. Thousands of sex and kink education videos featuring experts all over the world. Although there is a fee, the site offers free clips to give you an idea of whether it's what you want. PassionateU.com, their sister institution, posts videos about general sexuality.

Kink-Aware Professionals, ncsfreedom.org/resources/kink-aware-professionals-directory. If you're looking for a therapist, doctor or other professional who will not be judgmental of your kink interests, this is a great place to start your search.

LAW AND POLITICS

The National Coalition for Sexual Freedom (www.ncsfreedom.org) is a lobbying and legal support group for kinksters and others with nontraditional sexualities or relationships.They are also spearheading the "Consent Counts" project, which teaches standards for consent, and for managing consent problems, in a non-judgmental, kink-positive environment. Support them if you can; it's your freedoms they're protecting.

BDSM/KINK

The Artisan's Book of Fetishcraft: Patterns & Instructions for Creating Professional Fetishwear, Restraints & Equipment
John Huxley $27.95

Conquer Me: girl-to-girl wisdom about fulfilling your submissive desires
Kacie Cunningham $13.95

Family Jewels: A Guide to Male Genital Play and Torment
Hardy Haberman $12.95

Flogging
Joseph Bean $11.95

The Human Pony: A Guide for Owners, Trainers & Admirers
Rebecca Wilcox $27.95

The Mistress Manual: a good girl's guide to female dominance
Mistress Lorelei Powers $16.95

The (New and Improved) Loving Dominant
John Warren $16.95

The New Bottoming Book & The New Topping Book
Dossie Easton & Janet W. Hardy $14.95 ea.

Playing Well With Others: Your Field Guide to Discovering, Exploring & Navigating the Kink, Leather & BDSM Communities
Lee Harrington & Mollena Williams $19.95

Radical Ecstasy: SM Journeys to Transcendence
Dossie Easton & Janet W. Hardy $16.95

The Seductive Art of Japanese Bondage
Midori, photographs by Craig Morey $27.95

SM 101: A Realistic Introduction
Jay Wiseman $24.95

Spanking for Lovers
Janet W. Hardy $13.95

GENERAL SEXUALITY

DIY Porn Handbook: A How-To Guide to Documenting Our Own Sexual Revolution
Madison Young $15.95

The Explorer's Guide to Planet Orgasm
Annie Sprinkle $13.95

A Hand in the Bush: The Fine Art of Vaginal Fisting
Deborah Addington $13.95

The Jealousy Workbook: Exercises and Insights for Managing Open Relationships
Kathy Labriola $19.95

Love In Abundance: A Counselor's Advice on Open Relationships
Kathy Labriola $15.95

Miss Vera's Cross-Gender Fun for All
Veronica Vera $14.95

Tricks... To Please a Man & Tricks... To Please a Woman
Jay Wiseman $13.95 ea.

When Someone You Love Is Kinky
Dossie Easton & Catherine A. Liszt $15.95

TOYBAG GUIDES:
A Workshop In A Book $9.95 each

Age Play, by Lee "Bridgett" Harrington

Basic Rope Bondage, by Jay Wiseman

Chastity Play, by Miss Simone

Clips and Clamps, by Jack Rinella

Dungeon Emergencies & Supplies, by Jay Wiseman

Hot Wax and Temperature Play, by Spectrum

Playing With Taboo, by Mollena Williams

Greenery Press books and ebooks are available from your favorite on-line or brick-and-mortar bookstore or sex shop. If you are having trouble locating the book you want, please contact us at 541-683-0961.